# MAYUMU

# Filipino American Desserts Remixed

# MAYUMU

## Abi Balingit

**HARVEST**
*An Imprint of* WILLIAM MORROW

Turrones de Casoy MSG
Brownies (page 128)

To my parents. You told me,
"Bahala ka sa buhay mo!"
So I did.

# CONTENTS

# INTRODUCTION

My Filipino mother wasn't the type to bake Duncan Hines brownies or elaborate yellow cakes for my birthday parties. She always thought sugar-laden American desserts were too *mayumu*, which is the Kapampangan word for "sweet." Angelita Balingit did, however, love making cassava cakes and stirring large pots of maja blanca pudding for every family gathering. I helped her add condensed milk to the bowl, and she occasionally allowed me to try the leftovers that clung to the wooden spoon.

**W**hile these desserts have a special place in my heart, I let my palate roam free to not only appreciate Filipino flavors, but those of other cuisines around me. I grew up in the Bay Area and the Central Valley, where I would go to *paleterías* and *neverías* for my favorite mouthwatering mangonadas. These Mexican ice pop and ice cream stores were the only places I could get those frozen treats layered high with mango sorbet, Tajín, chamoy, and fresh mango. At my family's go-to Vietnamese spots, I'd beg my parents for some honeydew milk tea with boba to go along with my meal. I needed a refreshing drink in between hot spoonfuls of bright-red *bún bò Huế*, a spicy beef and pork noodle soup. As a kid, exploring the junk food aisles of 99 Ranch, one of the most prolific Asian supermarket chains based in California, made me crave chocolate Pocky, creamy White Rabbit candy, and crunchy Boy Bawang Cornick garlic-flavored corn nuts. Even though my mom didn't make me Pillsbury cookies, I snuck Little Debbie Oatmeal Creme Pies and Flamin' Hot Cheetos into the shopping cart when she wasn't looking.

From my childhood to my mid-twenties, one thing has remained the same: my insatiable desire for new combinations of sweet, salty, savory, sour, and umami in desserts. *Mayumu* is my story of what it means to be a Filipino American baker in New York, and to make sweets that taste like home in a tiny kitchen. When my now-agent, Emmy, replied to one of my Lao Gan Ma cupcake photos I posted on Twitter in September 2020, they asked if I was thinking of writing a cookbook. Up until that point, the thought had never crossed my mind. I was just a little baking blog that could. It was so early in the process of writing *The Dusky Kitchen* posts that I wasn't even sure if I had it in me to create so many of my own recipes. Not to get too meta, but what you're reading now is the culmination of all these efforts, luck, and also years of baking.

Although the recipes include some classic Filipino dessert staples and flavors, the ways in which they are presented or combined with other cuisines might be nowhere near traditional. You'll see my dad's luscious leche flan paired with the warm notes of chai masala (page 231). Instead of ube and jackfruit-flavored layers for *sapin-sapin*, I've offered a strawberry shortcake version of this glutinous rice cake (page 33). On the other side of the spectrum, I've also drawn inspiration from savory Filipino dishes like *kare-kare* and adobo for a couple of cookie recipes. Whether you're a novice baker or a pro, this cookbook invites you to embrace your own ingenuity and let go of some preconceptions of what is possible in both Filipino and American desserts. If you aren't familiar with the Filipino words peppered throughout the book, you will find them defined in the glossary (page 264).

There's a saying in Tagalog that many of us first-generation Filipino American kids have co-opted from our mothers: *Bahala ka sa buhay mo!* Roughly translated, it means "Do whatever with your life!" Strip away nanay's passive-aggressive tone, and it becomes an inspirational mantra. When you read the stories I've included from my own life, I hope they show that allowing yourself to be yourself is a journey. To do whatever you want is easy to say but sometimes harder in practice. Every time I look at myself in the mirror, I still see a work in progress. Despite these insecurities, recognizing that my relationships with my identity, food, family, and friends are constantly evolving has helped me become a better person and baker. Through moments of joy and even melancholy, I've been able to unlock memories that have led me to create the desserts you'll find in this book. As you read onward, I hope that my reflections on my past provide some insight on who I am now and, by extension, how these recipes came to be. I want you to let your imagination run wild when you're baking from this cookbook, and to have the confidence to create something *mayumu* in your own kitchen.

*Lemon Sunshine Uraro Cookies (page 171)*

# TINY KITCHEN ESSENTIALS

In the past five years, I've lived in three apartments all over Brooklyn with at least two roommates in each one. New York City living is notorious for small spaces, exorbitant rent prices, evil landlords, pest problems, etc. While living in tiny apartments and making do with even tinier kitchens has been less than ideal, it's still possible to create fantastic desserts in them.

**M**y biggest piece of advice is to look at the glass as half full when assessing your space. Every kitchen, no matter how big or small, is sacred. As a cook and baker who has grown accustomed to sharing a kitchen with multiple people, making it work also makes it feel more like home. When I was living with my parents and wanted to bake more, I encountered similar growing pains with their tendency to be territorial in the kitchen. Even if you live alone, you can still benefit from these tips and maximize the room you have to embark on any baking project. Here are some tips for those of us living in puny spaces and how to make baking as fun and efficient as possible in them:

**Having clear, open communication with your roommates is key for allocating enough time and space for baking.**

Baking in a tiny kitchen can be even more chaotic when you haven't established boundaries and expectations with the people you live with. Figuring out a cleaning regimen, allocating designated spaces for each person's food, and being mindful of one another's cooking schedules will set the foundation for smooth sailing. In addition, knowing what ingredients are fair game to share helps with maximizing space in your fridge and cabinets. For example, eggs and spices are all ingredients that my roommates and I consider to be communal.

**Inventory all your pantry essentials, especially when you're running low on certain ingredients.**

If you write down the stock you have of your ingredients, it helps to avoid the mistake of buying duplicates at the grocery store. Share the info with your roommates or family members and encourage them to add to that list. You will also find yourself less prone to completely running out of something midway through a recipe.

**Every surface is a place for opportunity.**

When you don't have room for a dining table, you have to be creative with where you can lay out ingredients and baked goods. I often cool freshly baked cupcakes on a wire rack on top of the TV stand when my island is otherwise occupied. I'll even pull out stools and use them as tiny tables.

**Clean as you go!**

Dirty dishes might be one of the biggest deterrents for baking that people can have, especially when an apartment doesn't come with a dishwasher. I dread having a massive pile of dishes to clean even before I start baking! Wash and dry bowls, utensils, etc., throughout the baking process so you don't leave yourself with a mountain of dishes at the end.

**Sometimes you have to take the L and wash dishes that aren't yours to expedite the process of working on a dessert.**

There are two choices in life: be petty or swallow the pride pill and move on. Personally, I can't cook or bake if there are already lots of dirty dishes in the sink. If there is a saucepan that's been used and the roommate who cooked with it has already left for work, I'm not going to throw a fit and wait for them to come home and wash it. I'll clean something myself if I have to, especially if it's the only one of something we have. Again, it's important to have clear communication with your roommates about cleaning dishes in a timely manner, but if you're in a time crunch, it's okay to expedite the process in whatever way you see fit.

**Reusing jars and containers for storage and organization is good for the planet and for your soul.**

My ancestors have been doing this since the dawn of time, and it really is a tradition for a reason. People joke about their families never throwing out a single container so they can repurpose it (e.g., the blue Royal Dansk Danish Butter Cookie tin for sewing supplies!), but this kind of innovation is so useful. I recently repurposed a potato chip can as a kitchen utensil holder, and takeout plastic containers can be washed and reused for storing leftover frosting. The possibilities are endless!

**There is no shame in using store-bought goods to execute a dessert.**

Whether you buy ready-made pie crust or ice cream from the grocery store, this is a no-judgment zone! It doesn't make you any less of a baker if you find ways to save time. If you want to rain check baking an element from scratch for when you're less stressed, by all means, do it.

**If you don't have a certain piece of equipment or a specialty ingredient, don't be afraid to phone a friend.**

You never know if a neighbor or a pal has a kitchen tool or niche ingredient you need for a baking project. If you feel like a certain piece of equipment or an ingredient is too expensive or not worth the kitchen space, I highly suggest asking around to borrow it. If they can't spare their Bundt cake pan or some cardamom pods, the worst they can say is no. Make sure to take good care of something on loan and return it in a timely manner; otherwise, it might get lost or damaged in your sea of supplies.

**Counting out loud as you measure ingredients helps you avoid making critical mistakes.**

There can be so many diversions when you're crammed into a kitchen that doesn't have a lot of square footage. You might be distracted by people watching TV in the living room or even by the sheer amount of multitasking you're doing for one recipe. I like to talk to myself in the kitchen, and counting out cups of flour helps with my memory. Your roommates might even hear you and help verify your measurements if you lose your train of thought.

**Mise en place can save you from a headache in the future.**

Measuring ingredients out beforehand and having them ready to go might seem like a pain when you're impatient to get the bake started, but it really does help in the long run. I cannot count the number of times that I've been halfway through a recipe and realized that I don't have x ingredient(s). To avoid having to do the mad dash to the bodega, mise en place before you start baking.

**Hooks, hooks, hooks!**

Having hooks on the kitchen wall for hanging up oven mitts, towels, and kitchen utensils really helps you remember where things are. Strong hooks on the side of a storage cart that can carry cast iron skillets are doing the Lord's work. When the space inside drawers and cabinets is already precious, I love utilizing hooks for freeing up shelves you might need for other items.

**Make sure you seal containers full of flour and other grains as tight as possible.**

I will never forget the Great Weevil Infestation of 2020 that plagued our apartment. My roommate noticed the black, slow-moving insects crawling around the floor, and they quickly infiltrated any loose bags of flour or grains. Much to my chagrin, we had to throw everything out. I have since moved all flour and grains to airtight containers with lids so we don't have to deal with this debacle ever again. Let this be a cautionary tale for you.

**Labels matter.**

Double-check expiration dates when you're using any ingredient. If your baking soda has been expired for five years, chances are that it will not help your banana bread rise in the slightest. Also, if you store leftovers in the fridge, use painter's tape and a Sharpie to label them. You will want to write down what it is and when it was made, so you don't forget. I've seen unlabeled things, which none of my roommates will claim and are too scared to chuck, lost in the abyss of both my fridge and freezer.

**Be sure to set your timer and take notes while baking.**

This tip might be simple and self-explanatory, but I have forgotten these steps in the past and it's always bitten me in the butt. When testing recipes, it's critical to note what deviations you've made from the original trial and how long it takes for it to bake. When you're overconfident about making mental notes, you'll be kicking yourself for not writing them down somewhere if you forget them. My writing tablet of choice is the iPhone Notes app.

**Normalize keeping equipment in unconventional places.**

When I was growing up, my parents used

the dishwasher solely as a drying rack. As an adult with maxed-out cabinet space, you'll see cardboard treat boxes strategically placed in a section of my living room. Sometimes, the kitchen is too crowded and you need to find other spots in your home for storage. If you don't have the budget or the space to build more shelving, make do with the open crevices and corners that you do have. Admittedly, there are some random cake decorating tools wedged underneath my bed too. I recommend making a note of where these items are, because you don't want to spend hours scrounging for them if you forget their hiding places.

**Online grocery stores are a godsend when you're in a pinch for time, but make sure you buy in bulk to maximize your order.**

If I don't want to trek to Queens or Chinatown for Asian ingredients, I will opt to order online from stores that deliver to my door. Since there is usually a minimum spend amount, I take some time to think about what other ingredients I need to get for meals throughout the week. Overall, you will save money and time that you would have spent tracking down ingredients in-person.

**Cutting a cake into slices and making individual portions will incentivize people to eat more of your desserts.**

If a baked good isn't already cut into portions, I've noticed that my roommates will be less inclined to eat it. I like texting our group chat that the dessert I've made is up for grabs so that they know I want them to try it. If it's too much work to slice up or too large, people will tend to forgo eating it. Although, if they have a sweet tooth, they will overcome any obstacle to have a bite!

**Sharing baked goods is caring.**

When you want to make a variety of baked goods in a short period of time, you and your roommates (and their respective partners) can only eat so many sweets. If you work in an office, I recommend giving them to coworkers. And if you still have servings to dole out, neighbors and friends will be happy to help. If all else fails, try to halve a recipe if you know the yield will be far too much for your household.

**Patience is underrated.**

While you can say that love is a special ingredient in all your baking, patience is really important when you're in the kitchen. Whether it's your first time or seventeenth time making a dessert, be kind to yourself if something goes wrong. Don't let one bad bake keep you from ever baking again! In a lot of ways, I treat baking like self-care. The act of it allows me to take deep breaths, slow down, and focus on a recipe. With a little patience, you can become a great baker.

# FILIPINO PANTRY
*essentials*

JACKFRUIT
IN SYRUP

NET WT 20oz DR WT 8.1oz

BUENAS

COCONUT SPORT
MACAPUNO STRING

NET WT 12oz (340g)

LINGAYEN

SAUTEED
SHRIMP FRY

NET WT 340g / 12oz

SOY SAUCE
SAUCE DE SOJA

BUTTERFLY

Lychee
FLAVOR

BUTTERFLY

Pandan
FLAVOR

BUTTERFLY

Ube
FLAVOR

KAONG

Sugar
Palm
Fruit
IN SYRUP

Angelina

SHREDDED
YOUNG COCONUT
~ Buko ~

Net Weight: 16 oz (454 g)

KEEP FROZEN

POWDERED
PURPLE YAM

UBE

PINOY FIESTA

GRATED PURPLE YAM
(Kinayod na Ube)

Carabao's Milk

HALO-HALO

Fruit Mix
and
Beans
IN SYRUP

Lucia

PURE CHINESE
LYE WATER

NET WT | PONDS NET 341 g

Tropics
Since 1970

Banana
Leaves

NATA DE COCO

Coconut
Gel
IN SYRUP

FROZEN
PANDAN LEAVES

Tropics

UBE HALAYA
PURPLE YAM JAM

NET WT 12oz

Classic
HOT CHOCOLATE
TABLEA    10 Cacao Tablets    NET WT 7.05 OZ (200g)

ITLOG NA MAALAT

Cooked Salted Duck Egg

Rufina
PATIS

FISH SAUCE

NET CONTENTS 750 ML (1.508 PT)

# Recommended Brands for Specialty Filipino Ingredients

**You can usually find these ingredients at your local Filipino or Asian grocery store, especially a chain like Seafood City. If you want to order them online, Sarap Now and Weee! offer nationwide delivery.**

**Wang Derm Frozen Pandan Leaves**

Pandan, or screwpine, leaves have a grassy aroma and lend vanilla and coconut flavors to both savory and sweet Southeast Asian dishes. While it's more difficult to come across these fresh, it's easy to thaw frozen pandan leaves, tie them in a knot, and let them steep in any liquid.

**Tropics Frozen Banana Leaves**

Banana leaves can be used for wrapping food for grilling, steaming, or baking. I love the earthy flavor that you get from cooking anything in banana leaves. For Filipino feasts, food can be served on top of banana leaves for a beautiful presentation.

**Kapuso Nata de Coco**

Nata de coco, or coconut gel, is a sweet byproduct of fermenting coconut water. Jars of nata de coco are usually located in the canned section of Filipino grocery stores. You will typically find these chewy cubes in classic Filipino desserts like buko pandan salad, halo-halo, and fruit salad. If you've ever asked for lychee jellies to add to your bubble tea order, they are usually made of nata de coco.

**Kapuso Kaong**

Kaong is the chewy bean-shaped fruit of the sugar palm tree. Kaong is normally translucent white, but you can find jars of red- and green-colored varieties to add to chilled Filipino desserts much like the ones that have nata de coco.

**Buenas Macapuno Strings**

Macapuno, or coconut sport, strings are the translucent and sweet endosperm of a special type of coconut. The meat is jellylike, which is where it differs from regular coconut. You can find jars of macapuno preserved in syrup at your local Filipino supermarket. Ube macapuno is a popular flavor combination in the Philippines.

**Lucia Yellow Jackfruit**

Unlike the green jackfruit in brine that is often used for savory dishes, yellow jackfruit can be found canned in syrup and is very sweet. It is a tropical fruit with flavors reminiscent of pineapple and banana, and the pods can be pulled apart like string cheese. Turon is a Filipino snack consisting of saba banana and strips of yellow jackfruit rolled in a spring roll wrapper, then fried and coated in caramel.

**Kapuso Halo-Halo Mix**

These jars filled with a mixture of sweetened beans, nata de coco, kaong, macapuno strings, and yellow jackfruit make up the bulk of halo-halo, the quintessential Filipino shaved ice dessert. If you spoon some of this mix over ice, evaporated milk, and ice cream in cups, you can have multiple servings of halo-halo to share with family and friends.

**Pinoy Fiesta Frozen Grated Ube**

Fresh purple yam is hard to come by, but the frozen grated version is perfect for making ube halaya. With the addition of milk and sugar, it cooks down to a thick jam.

**Giron Foods Powdered Ube**

When I can't find frozen grated ube, the powdered version is a great alternative. However, it takes a bit more time and water to rehydrate this ube. You'll usually find it in bags at Filipino grocery stores.

**Tropics Ube Halaya**

There is a whole recipe section on three ways to make ube halaya in this book. However, in a pinch, you can always buy it premade in a jar. I like to have a dollop of it on top of halo-halo or even smear it on toasted bread.

**Butterfly Brand Extracts Ube, Pandan, and Lychee**

In order to enhance the flavor of certain desserts, Butterfly Brand's assortment of extracts comes in handy. These ube and pandan extracts punch up purple and green colors, respectively, in different treats. Lychee extract in my signature madeleine recipe lends a lot of flavor without fresh lychees' excess moisture.

**Angelina Frozen Shredded Buko**

Getting the meat out of fresh buko is an endeavor in itself! If you don't want to bust out the machete, I recommend buying frozen and shredded young coconut. Using thawed buko is the fastest way of making the filling for buko pie.

**Marca Piña Soy Sauce**

Filipino soy sauce, also called toyo, is incomparable. It's so much darker and saltier than other varieties. I look for the pineapples on the label of Marca Piña soy sauce bottles because it's my dad's first choice for cooking adobo.

**Maria's Authentic Bulacan Sweets Carabao Milk**

Carabao is a type of water buffalo native to the Philippines. Carabaos produce milk that is much creamier and contains more butterfat than cow milk. It makes puddings, cheeses, and other sweets much more decadent. I get bottles of carabao milk shipped specifically from Maria's Authentic Bulacan Sweets, a purveyor in Queens.

**Lingayen Spicy Sautéed Bagoong**

Bagoong alamang is a Filipino fermented shrimp paste, which is sautéed and takes on a reddish-brown color. You can find the spicy version in a jar and commonly used as a condiment for kare-kare or green mangoes. Bagoong isda refers to a different variation of the condiment made with fermented fish.

**Alfonso's Hot Chocolate Tablea**

Tablea are roasted cacao tablets that get dissolved in milk for Filipino hot chocolate, called tsokolate. They can also be used in champorado for flavoring the rice porridge. Each package usually comes with ten tablea.

**Homei Cooked Salted Duck Eggs**

You can find cooked salted duck eggs at any Asian supermarket. While they do taste great whole in tomato salads with a splash of vinegar, the yolks have the most potent flavor and are especially salty. I was so excited to see salted duck egg ice cream in the Philippines.

**Lucia Lye Water**

Lye water is a food-grade alkaline solution used in small amounts for various kakanin recipes like kutsinta and pichi-pichi. It gives the rice cakes their distinctive chewy texture. Wear gloves when using lye water, because it is caustic, and you should never swallow it straight from the bottle.

**Rufina Patis**

Filipino fish sauce is a pungent, dark brown condiment that has a strong umami flavor. One of my earliest memories is seeing my aunt dip green apple slices in patis for a midday snack. It adds a hit of salt to whatever you're fixing up in the kitchen.

*Mommy's Ginataang Bilo-Bilo (page 257)*

Raspberry & Chamoy
Pichi-Pichi (page 38)

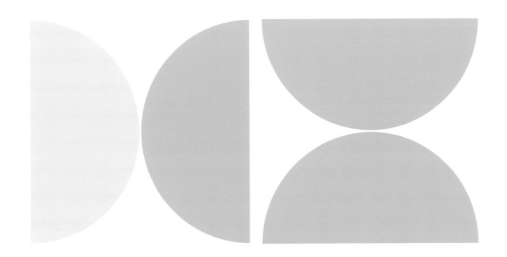

# PART I
## Pampanga, Philippines

*Once upon a Time in . . .*
*Pampanga*

**My parents are from Pampanga, one of the seven provinces in Central Luzon. Pampanga is heralded as the culinary capital of the Philippines. Even when I would tell other Filipinos about my parents' origins, the first thing they would say is that Pampanga has the best cooks. Across the board, I would say that my family's prowess in the kitchen is unmatched.**

**A**s *a kid,* I couldn't wrap my brain around how densely the branches of my family tree extend out on both sides. To this day, I run out of fingers and toes after trying to count how many cousins I have. My dad, Arnel Balingit, is the second eldest of six, while my mom is the second youngest of seven. To me, it always seemed like a mind-boggling number of siblings, even if the counts are standard for a TLC reality show. Both my parents would say that they didn't have much money growing up, but they had carefree childhoods. My dad loves to tell me stories of forgoing schoolwork to blissfully suck on fresh sugarcane stalks. Lolo Hugo, my grandfather on my dad's side, was a farmer, and Lola Undi was a stay-at-home mom. Lolo Benjie, my grandfather on my mom's side, was a tailor, while Lola Mercy also helped raise the kids.

During the tumultuous years when the Philippines was under martial law, both my parents went to college at different universities and received BS degrees in commerce. After they graduated, my dad met my mom by chance in 1985 while hanging out with mutual friends. At the time, my dad was an Overseas Filipino Worker (OFW) in Saudi Arabia and worked abroad in order to send money back home. He came back from the Middle East in 1987 to officially start courting my mom. Apparently, my dad came to visit my mom in the office and brought her flowers and chocolate with a note that read "I like you." My mom was head over heels for him since he looked like Gabby Concepcion, a popular Filipino actor. It was a short visit to Pampanga since he was due back at his administrative job in Saudi Arabia. For the next two years, they sent each other letters and voice tapes.

Through a series of petitions from my mom's oldest sister, Auntie Flor, who was the first

working. He applied for a visitor's visa three times in the span of nine months before he was accepted. He arrived in San Jose to be with my mom for good in December 1992, two weeks after my sister Ginelle was born.

To a degree, both of my parents experienced a form of culture shock. Funnily enough, my mom could not get over seeing white families throw birthday parties with just pepperoni pizza slices to offer for the kids' dinner. She still harps on how birthday celebrants should treat their guests with a bounty of food that includes meal options galore. While I was growing up, my mom always took pride in showing off our dining room table covered in aluminum trays filled with crispy lumpia, pork BBQ skewers glistening with fat, mounds of white rice, and countless other dishes for our birthday parties. My dad found that living in America was way less restrictive than being in Saudi Arabia. He enjoyed the freedom of not worrying about specific laws regarding the

to make it to California, my mom's side of the family immigrated to America in waves. Lolo Benjie flew into San Francisco in December 1982. Uncle Cris made the move in November 1989. My mom was on the same flight as three of her other siblings, Uncle Tan, Uncle Benjie, and Uncle Jones, along with Lola Mercy, in December 1989. Auntie Rina, one of my mom's older sisters, was her only sibling who remained in the Philippines for seven more years until joining the rest of the family in San Jose. My mom promised my dad that she would come back to the Philippines after a year to get married, but my strict Lola Mercy asked her to extend this waiting period by another year. On March 27, 1992, my parents finally had their no-frills wedding officiated by Archbishop Aniceto. The church ceremony was very small, and my mom wore a subdued, off-the-shoulder white dress complete with her permed hair. Even though she didn't go for a glitzy look, she looked exquisite. After the nuptials, my mom flew back to California, while my dad had to return to Saudi Arabia to continue

practice of religion and how to dress. They both observed that Americans moved so fast, were stressed constantly, and talked a mile a minute. Overall, they thought that the pace of life was much slower in the Philippines.

No matter how different their surroundings were, my mom and dad turned to Filipino comfort food for a taste of the familiar. While living in the same household as our extended family, my parents, Lolo Benjie, and Lola Mercy cooked enough food for everyone to share. The communal pot was the size of a witch's cauldron, and each person served their specialty out of it. My dad opted to cook a hearty Kapampangan stew called *asado*, which is made of beef tongue braised in a piquant blend of tomato sauce, soy sauce, and lemon juice. Lola Mercy's *burong mustasa*, or pickled mustard greens, acted as a sour complement to fried, marinated milkfish and rice. Lolo Benjie would often make an especially garlicky rendition of *dinuguan*, a pork blood and vinegar stew. My mom usually helmed the dessert division, and her earliest memory in San Jose was making *yema*. She painstakingly enrobed each of these egg custard balls in a layer of caramel. Whenever you took a bite of the yema, the hardened sugar coating created a wonderful textural contrast to the soft, rich candy. My family's penchant for sour, sweet, and fishy flavors did not skip my generation. I

appreciate that I inherited their love for Filipino cuisine, and that they didn't just give me cold Pizza Hut for dinner.

Outside of the home, my parents saw America as the land of opportunity. In contrast to the financial hardships they faced in the Philippines, they thought it was more feasible to make a better living here. When my mom first moved, she applied at a temp agency and eventually landed a full-time job in 1990. She worked in the accounts payable department at a fastener supplier company for seven years and then at a health insurance company called Lifeguard for five years. After a stint as a stay-at-home father, my dad also joined the workforce. From 1996 to 1999, my dad assembled machine parts for Komag, Inc. He helped this company manufacture magnetic discs for computer hard drives. It was his quick foray into the hardware sector of the Silicon Valley. Since my parents' relationship started off long-distance, they were happy to be together to raise Ginelle; my younger sister, Argeli; and me after their time apart. It also helped that they shared a home with my mom's extended family members, who babysat us while my parents were busy at work. I know it would've been so difficult if they'd had to navigate not only a new continent but also parenthood alone.

# JAMS, SYRUPS & TOPPINGS

Some desserts wouldn't be complete without these fillings or final garnishes. They can turn a good dish into an exceptional one. These recipes are foundational for certain others in this book.

# Ube Halaya, Three Ways

Ube halaya lends a richer ube flavor to desserts than extract alone. *Halaya* comes from the Spanish word *jalea*, which means "jam" in English. While you can eat ube halaya as a dessert by itself, it's often used as a topping for halo-halo or as a key ingredient in an ube chiffon cake. Even though you can always buy jars of ube jam at your local Filipino grocery store, you can make a more delicious version at home.

Fresh ube is quite difficult to find, so I've come up with three versions using ube in different forms. The first two, frozen and powdered, are fairly traditional, and the last one is definitely the most experimental of the trio. Since you have to rehydrate the ube powder for the second method, it can take upward of an hour of cooking on the stovetop. If you can't find frozen grated ube, this method–though time-intensive–is worth making for a comparable result. Ube Pillow Butter, the third halaya, has a subtle saltiness and slick mouthfeel to it. You've heard of speculoos cookie butter, but did you know that you can turn almost anything into butter? I love Ube Pillows, which are sweet ube-filled crackers produced by Oishi. If you can resist snacking on them, you can grind them up and turn the crumbs into a luscious spread.

People commonly mistake Okinawan sweet potatoes and taro for ube, but they all come from different families of root vegetables. It's rare to find fresh ube at all in the United States, and if it is available, it usually comes at a hefty price per pound. Ube is moist on the inside and sweet, and has a delicate flavor that is a cross between vanilla and pistachio. I've seen ube take over Instagram, mostly because of the vivid purple color it lends to desserts.

Ube, which is a yam native to the Philippines, typically has a dark brown skin reminiscent of tree bark. There are multiple varieties of ube, and the most popular and prized one is *kinampay*, which is specifically grown in Bohol. It's especially fragrant and sweet, and sacred to the people living in Bohol. Ranging from a mix of purple-white, lilac, and deep purple, ube flesh comes in so many shades of purple.

The first time I ever saw ube being grown in real life was actually in Brooklyn. A couple months ago, my boyfriend's best friend, Stephen, bought a live ube plant from Etsy and planted it in his backyard in Greenpoint. When he showed me the beautiful vines growing from the tuber, I couldn't stop fawning over the stunning purple-green color of the leaves. My jaw dropped when I saw them, and it just felt like a mini miracle seeing a piece of the motherland here in New York. I have yet to try his ube since it takes five to seven months for it to be harvested, but I cannot wait to taste it.

UBE PLANT
(DIOSCOREA ALATA)

# Frozen Ube Halaya

## Makes 4½ cups

1 (16-ounce) package frozen grated ube,
thawed but not drained of liquid

1 (14-ounce) can sweetened condensed milk

1 (13.5-ounce) can unsweetened, full-fat coconut milk

½ teaspoon kosher salt

4 tablespoons (½ stick) unsalted butter

1 teaspoon ube extract

———

**1**  In a medium saucepan, stir the grated ube,
condensed milk, coconut milk, and salt over low heat.
Continue to cook, stirring constantly with a rubber
spatula, for 15 minutes as it comes to a boil. The
mixture should start pulling away from the sides of the
pan as you stir. Cook until the mixture is thickened
to the point that the rubber spatula will stand upright
on its own if stuck in the jam, an additional 4 to
5 minutes.

**2**  Turn off the heat and stir in the butter and ube
extract, until the butter is melted and the mixture is
smooth, 1 to 2 minutes.

**3**  Cool at room temperature and then store in an
airtight container in the fridge for up to 2 weeks. When
you're ready to use the jam, it is best eaten cold.

# Powdered Ube Halaya

## Makes 4½ cups

1 (4.06-ounce) package powdered ube

1 (14-ounce) can sweetened condensed milk

1 (13.5-ounce) can unsweetened, full-fat coconut milk

2 tablespoons packed dark brown sugar

½ teaspoon kosher salt

4 tablespoons (½ stick) unsalted butter

1 teaspoon ube extract

———

**1**  In a medium saucepan, simmer the powdered
ube and 3 cups water over low heat until the ube is
rehydrated, 7 to 9 minutes.

**2**  Stir in the condensed milk, coconut milk, brown
sugar, and salt. Continue to cook, stirring frequently
with a rubber spatula, until the mixture thickens to the
consistency of mashed potatoes, 60 to 65 minutes.
Stirring is vital to keeping the halaya from burning at
the bottom of the pan!

**3**  Turn off the heat and stir in the butter and ube
extract until the butter is melted and the mixture is
smooth, 1 to 2 minutes.

**4**  Cool at room temperature and then store in an
airtight container in the fridge for up to 2 weeks. When
you're ready to use the jam, it is best eaten cold.

# Ube Pillow Butter

*Makes 2 cups*

1½ cups ube pillows
¼ cup light corn syrup
½ teaspoon kosher salt
I cup coconut oil
2 teaspoons ube extract

**1**   Grind the ube pillows in a food processor for 10 to 15 pulses, until they become fine crumbs.

**2**   Combine the ube pillow crumbs, ²/₃ cup water, the corn syrup, and salt in a medium saucepan. Cook over medium-high heat, stirring frequently with a rubber spatula, until the crumbs dissolve and the mixture reaches a boil, 2 to 3 minutes.

**3**   Turn off the heat and transfer the contents of the saucepan to a blender. Add in coconut oil and ube extract, then blend on medium-high until the mixture is smooth, 4 to 5 minutes.

**4**   Pour the mixture into a large glass jar and then cool at room temperature for 10 minutes. Cover the jar with a lid. Chill in the fridge for 30 minutes for the butter to solidify, take it out to give it a quick stir, and then refrigerate for another 30 minutes.

**5**   You can take the jar out, stir the contents, and serve at room temperature when it has softened to an optimal spreading consistency. Store any leftover butter, refrigerated in the sealed jar, for up to I week.

*Ube Melon Pandesal (page 193)*

# Matamis na Bao

*Makes ½ cup*

Matamis na bao, alternatively called minatamis na bao, is a rich coconut jam. You'll often see it spread on warm pandesal for breakfast. I like to use matamis na bao as a filling between two shortbread cookies for my take on alfajores. Similar to kaya jam, it's also flavored with pandan leaves, but it doesn't require eggs. After chilling in the fridge, it has a creamy, thick consistency. While most recipes use brown sugar, I love using coconut palm sugar for my matamis na bao because it makes it slightly earthy.

* 1 (13.5-ounce) can unsweetened, full-fat coconut milk
* 2 frozen pandan leaves, thawed and tied into knots
* ¾ cup coconut palm sugar

1   In a medium saucepan, combine the coconut milk, pandan leaves, and sugar. Cook over medium-high heat, stirring occasionally with a rubber spatula, until the mixture starts to boil, 4 to 5 minutes. Once the mixture is boiling, immediately reduce the heat to low. Continue to cook, stirring frequently, and remove the pandan knots at 20 minutes of total cook time.

2   Cook until the jam thickens and darkens, another 10 to 12 minutes. It should have the consistency of a caramel sauce.

3   Turn off the heat and transfer the jam to a glass jar. Allow to cool to room temperature and then place in the fridge. The jam will continue to thicken as it chills. Serve once it is spreadable. Store any leftovers in the refrigerator for up to 1 week.

# Caramelized Banana & Jackfruit Jam

*Makes 4 cups*

Imagine if you could take the essence of turon and boil it down into a condiment to slather on toast, pastries, and everything in between. Turon, the classic Filipino fried spring rolls filled with saba banana, brown sugar, and jackfruit, take some work to fry, and aren't available at the drop of a hat. This caramelized banana and jackfruit jam is the soft, spreadable answer to that prayer of having a taste of turon you can put on anything. By cooking down ripe banana and jackfruit in a vat of caramel, you're able to achieve the flavor of turon (minus the crunch of the crispy wrapper). Adding rum at the end gives it a bit of a bananas Foster taste and feel. When I close my eyes after taking a bite of this jam, I feel like I've been transported back to family parties in San Jose, where I monopolized whichever table housed the big aluminum tray of turon. I like to use this jam for a tropical turon linzer cookie recipe (page 175) that's perfect for a Christmas cookie box.

* 1¾ cups granulated sugar
* 2¾ cups mashed ripe banana (about 5 medium bananas)
* 1 (20-ounce) can yellow jackfruit in syrup, drained and minced
* ¼ teaspoon kosher salt
* 1 tablespoon fresh lemon juice
* 1 tablespoon dark rum

1   In a medium saucepan, place the sugar over low heat. Once the sugar starts to dissolve, stir frequently with a rubber spatula until the mixture completely liquifies and is a golden-brown color, 20 to 25 minutes.

2   Immediately pour the mashed bananas into the saucepan and stir until combined with the caramel. Don't be alarmed if the caramel starts to harden! It will remelt as you stir the mixture.

3   Simmer the banana mixture until it thickens slightly and the caramel is melted again, 8 to 10 minutes.

4   Stir in the minced jackfruit, salt, lemon juice, and rum. Clip a candy thermometer to the saucepan. Cook until the jam has reduced by one third and the temperature is between 210°F and 220°F, an additional 10 to 15 minutes. Turn off the heat.

5   Transfer the jam to a medium bowl and let cool completely at room temperature. Seal the bowl with a lid and store in the fridge for up to 2 weeks.

# Arnibal

*Makes 1½ cups*

**Arnibal is a simple syrup that requires only two ingredients: water and brown sugar. You'll most commonly see it poured over taho (see page 239), but it's versatile enough to use in any beverage or cocktail. Play around with adding ingredients like fresh pandan leaves or different extracts to switch up the flavor profile.**

* 1 cup packed dark brown sugar

1   Combine 1 cup water and the dark brown sugar in a small saucepan. Cook over medium-high heat, stirring occasionally with a wooden spoon until the mixture comes to a boil.

2   Reduce the heat to low and continue to simmer for 2 to 3 minutes, or until the sugar is completely dissolved. Turn off the heat.

3   Pour the arnibal into a large glass jar and let it cool at room temperature. Use as you would a simple syrup in your favorite beverages. After sealing the glass jar with a lid, you can store the arnibal in the fridge for up to 3 weeks.

# Peach Mango Compote

*Makes 2 cups*

Throughout my childhood and even up to now, I feel like Jollibee has been an indomitable pop culture icon. The red and yellow bee mascot has spawned memes that will forever be part of my psyche. The eponymous food chain has locations all over the world, and is known for offering Filipino spaghetti and fried chicken. When the first location in Manhattan opened in 2018, I remember there were bouncers at the door for crowd control because the lines were so long.

Besides the savory items on the menu, the one thing that I always get at Jollibee is the peach mango pie. If you don't want to trek to your local Jollibee, this peach mango compote is a lovely addition to any dessert. It's almost good enough to eat alone by the spoonful, especially if you're able to find Carabao, Champagne, or Ataulfo mangoes for it.

* 4 peaches, peeled and cut into 1/2-inch dice (2 cups)
* 4 medium mangoes, peeled and cut into 1/2-inch dice (2 cups)
* 2/3 cup sugar
* 2 tablespoons fresh lemon juice

1   Place the peaches, mangoes, sugar, and lemon juice in a medium saucepan. Stir with a wooden spoon and cook over medium-high heat until the mixture reaches a boil.

2   Reduce the heat to low and simmer, stirring occasionally, until most of the liquid has evaporated, 10 to 15 minutes. Remove from the heat.

3   Serve the compote warm or chilled. Store in an airtight container in the fridge for up to 1 week. If you choose to warm leftover compote, you can gently heat it over low heat in a saucepan to get it to your desired temperature.

# Latik
# (Toasted Coconut Curds)

*Makes 1 cup*

There's a plethora of kakanin (rice cakes) that are sprinkled with toasted coconut curds called latik. Making latik is a labor of love, but well worth it. Although this recipe only uses one ingredient, it takes some patience to wait for the coconut cream to boil and later separate. Essentially, the curds fry in their own oil and you're left with slightly salty, crumbly coconut bits that you can use as a topping. If you don't have coconut cream, you can alternatively use coconut milk. Just note that the yield will be much less than the original recipe since coconut cream has more solids.

* 1 (33.8-ounce) carton coconut cream

1   Pour the coconut cream into a large saucepan and bring it to a boil over medium-high heat. Immediately reduce the heat to low and stir occasionally with a wooden spoon to prevent the cream from boiling over. Continue to cook as the oil and solids start to separate, stirring frequently to make sure nothing is burning at the bottom of the pan. Keep cooking until the curds are a golden-brown color, 65 to 75 minutes.

2   Once they're done cooking, turn off the heat and strain the coconut oil from the saucepan using a large sieve. You can save the oil at room temperature in a glass jar with a lid for up to 2 days; you will be left with latik in the strainer.

3   Store the latik in an airtight container in the fridge for up to 1 week if not immediately using it.

# KAKANIN

Kakanin encompasses an assortment of delicacies made from rice and coconut milk and is the cornerstone of Filipino desserts. The name comes from the word *kanin*, which means "rice," but there are also some varieties that have cassava. Kakanin were historically precolonial offerings to the gods, but are now commonly offered as merienda snacks for family and friends.

# Strawberry Shortcake Sapin-Sapin (Layered Rice Cake)

*Makes 18 mini sapin-sapin*

Sapin-sapin is a tri-layered rice cake that traditionally features tropical flavors, but I believe that it's a vehicle for a whole host of variations. Any time there is a family holiday party or special occasion, I look forward to getting my tithe of sapin-sapin from the dessert table. Each chewy layer is so vibrant—typically colored purple, white, or orange to correspond with the flavors of ube, macapuno, or jackfruit.

For my take on sapin-sapin, I was inspired by my childhood favorite Good Humor strawberry shortcake bars. I used to gaze longingly out the window whenever the ice cream truck circled my block and played "Frosty the Snowman" in the middle of July. Here, there's a red layer for strawberry, white for vanilla, and brown for molasses. The latik (toasted coconut curds) on top are crunchy, nutty, and slightly salty, and the addition of freeze-dried strawberry helps to mimic the cake crumbs on the original strawberry shortcake bars with a touch more tropical flavor from the coconut. Instead of latik, you can use crushed shortbread for a similar textural component.

* 2 tablespoons coconut oil, melted, for brushing
* 1½ cups glutinous rice flour
* ½ cup rice flour
* 1 cup sugar
* 1 (13.5-ounce) can unsweetened, full-fat coconut milk
* ¼ cup organic strawberry preserves
* 2 to 3 drops red gel food coloring
* 1 teaspoon vanilla extract
* 2 tablespoons robust molasses
* ⅛ teaspoon cinnamon
* 1 ounce freeze-dried strawberries
* 3 tablespoons Latik (Toasted Coconut Curds, page 30)

1    Prepare a steamer by filling a large pot with 2 inches of water and fitting the pot with a steel steaming rack. Bring the water to a boil over medium-high heat. Using a pastry brush, grease 18 aluminum egg tart molds with the coconut oil. Set aside.

2    Whisk the glutinous rice flour, rice flour, sugar, and coconut milk together in a large bowl until the mixture is smooth. Divide the mixture evenly among three small bowls.

3    In the first bowl, mix in the strawberry preserves and red gel food coloring. In the second

*Continued*

## STRAWBERRY SHORTCAKE ICE CREAM BAR

## STRAWBERRY SHORTCAKE

## SAPIN-SAPIN

bowl, mix in the vanilla. In the third bowl, mix in the molasses and cinnamon. Set aside.

4   Pour I tablespoon of the strawberry mixture into each prepared mold. Place the molds on the steaming rack and cover the pot with a lid. Depending on the size of your steamer, you may have to steam the sapin-sapin in multiple batches and add more water as you go. Steam for about 5 minutes, or until the layer is set and no longer liquid.

5   Remove the lid, pour I tablespoon of the vanilla mixture over each of the strawberry layers, and cover with the lid again. Steam for another 5 minutes.

6   Remove the lid, pour I tablespoon of the molasses mixture over each of the vanilla layers, and cover with the lid again. Steam for 5 minutes, or until the last layer is set and firm to the touch. Using tongs, remove the molds from the steamer and let them cool completely at room temperature.

7   In the bowl of a food processor, blitz the freeze-dried strawberries until they turn into a powder. Set aside.

8   Use a small rubber spatula to gently loosen the sapin-sapin from their molds. Invert upside down on a plate with the strawberry layer facing up. To serve, top each sapin-sapin with $1/2$ teaspoon of the latik and $1/4$ teaspoon of the freeze-dried strawberry powder. If not serving immediately, store the sapin-sapin in an airtight container in the fridge for up to 3 days.

# Vanilla Bean Cassava Cake with Milk Candy Custard Topping

*Makes 10 servings*

Whenever my parents took me to 99 Ranch, our favorite Asian supermarket, I always came back home with a bag of White Rabbit candy. No matter how much they'd get stuck in my teeth, I'd keep reaching for more. The Chinese milk candy has such a grip on our generation that there's White Rabbit–flavored everything: ice cream, Swiss rolls, cocktails, you name it! For my cassava cake recipe, melting down White Rabbit imparts all of the candy's flavor into the topping, and it marries well with the vanilla bean in the base. The cake itself is fork-tender, with a bit of a chew from the starchiness of the cassava.

* 1 frozen banana leaf, rinsed and thawed (or parchment paper in a pinch)
* Nonstick spray
* 1 (16-ounce) package frozen grated cassava, thawed
* 2 large eggs, at room temperature
* 1½ cups unsweetened, full-fat coconut milk
* 1 cup sweetened condensed milk
* 1 (12-ounce) can evaporated milk
* 2 tablespoons unsalted butter, melted
* ½ teaspoon kosher salt
* 1½ teaspoons vanilla bean paste (see Note)
* 10 White Rabbit candies
* 1 tablespoon cornstarch
* 2 large egg yolks, at room temperature

*Note: Instead of vanilla bean paste, you can use the seeds scraped from a whole vanilla bean or 1½ teaspoons vanilla extract.*

1   Position a rack in the middle of the oven and preheat the oven to 350°F. Wipe down the banana leaf and cut out a 14-inch square with kitchen scissors. Line a 10¼-inch cast iron skillet with the banana leaf. Coat with nonstick spray and set aside.

2   For the cake, combine the thawed cassava, eggs, ¾ cup of the coconut milk, ½ cup of the condensed milk, 1 cup plus 2 tablespoons of the evaporated milk, the melted butter, salt, and vanilla bean paste in a large bowl. Whisk until the batter is smooth. Pour the mixture into the lined skillet and bake for 40 to 45 minutes, or until it has set and is no longer liquid. Take the skillet out of the oven and set on a wire rack to cool while you make the topping.

3   For the topping, place the White Rabbit candies and ¾ cup of the coconut milk in a

*Continued*

small saucepan. Cook over medium-low heat, stirring frequently with a rubber spatula, until the candies are completely dissolved in the milk, 3 to 4 minutes. Turn off the heat. Add the remaining $1/2$ cup of the condensed milk, the remaining $1/4$ cup plus 2 tablespoons evaporated milk, and the cornstarch to the saucepan.

4   In a small bowl, whisk the egg yolks until lightly beaten. Ladle $1/4$ cup of the White Rabbit mixture into the bowl and whisk quickly to temper the yolks. Transfer the contents of the small bowl into the saucepan and mix with the other ingredients until smooth. Pour the mixture on top of the cassava cake.

5   Place the cake back in the oven and bake for an additional 22 to 25 minutes, or until the topping is set. Turn the oven to broil for 1 to 3 minutes, until the topping develops some brown spots and looks bubbly. Transfer the cake to a wire rack to cool and serve at room temperature. Store leftover cake in an airtight container in the fridge for up to 1 week.

# Raspberry & Chamoy Pichi-Pichi

### *Makes 28 pichi-pichi*

*Pichi-pichi* have a very simple base: lye water, sugar, cassava, and tap water. You can buy food-grade lye water from Asian grocery stores, but be careful while handling because it is caustic. Once the pichi-pichi mixture is steamed in egg tart molds, it becomes sticky and gelatinous. I love eating this circular kakanin for a midday snack once they're cooled then coated with grated coconut. My raspberry and chamoy pichi-pichi deviate from traditional recipes that use pandan or ube for additional flavoring.

Chamoy is a Mexican condiment that is made from chiles and pickled fruit, which makes it alluringly sweet, sour, salty, and spicy. It's easy to purchase bottles of chamoy online or at the grocery store, often in the fruit section. My first memory of chamoy is seeing the sauce doused all over a mangonada, which is a refreshing dessert layered with mango sorbet, fresh mango, and Tajín. The fresh raspberry puree reserved for the other half of the recipe is a superb foil to the chamoy pichi-pichi. The raspberry zing really pulls through even after the pichi-pichi have been steamed. After they've cooled, the pink and red pichi-pichi are rolled in unsweetened shredded coconut. They remind me of little Hostess Sno Balls (except they're not sickly sweet!).

* Nonstick spray
* I cup frozen grated cassava, thawed
* ½ cup sugar
* ½ teaspoon lye water (see page 14)
* 2 tablespoons fresh raspberry puree
* 2 tablespoons chamoy
* ¾ cup unsweetened shredded coconut

1   Prepare a steamer by filling a large pot with 2 inches of water and fitting the pot with a steel steaming rack. Bring the water to a boil over medium-high heat. Grease 28 cavities of silicone mini muffin molds with nonstick spray. Line a baking sheet with parchment paper. Set aside.

2   In a large measuring cup, whisk the thawed cassava, sugar, ½ cup plus 2 tablespoons water, and the lye water until well combined.

3   Divide the mixture between two small bowls. Add the raspberry puree to one of the bowls

*Continued*

and whisk until smooth. Add the chamoy to the second bowl and whisk until smooth. Fill 14 of the muffin cavities with 1 tablespoon of the raspberry mixture. Fill each of the remaining 14 cavities with 1 tablespoon of the chamoy mixture.

4   Place the molds on the steaming rack and cover the pot with a lid. Depending on the size of your steamer, you may have to steam the pichi-pichi in multiple batches and add more water as you go. Steam for 10 to 15 minutes, or until the pichi-pichi have set and are translucent.

5   Using tongs, remove the molds from the steamer and allow them to cool for 1 minute before inverting the pichi-pichi onto the lined baking sheet. Repeat this process until all the pichi-pichi are cooked and unmolded.

6   Place the coconut in a small bowl. Roll each pichi-pichi in the coconut until evenly coated. Put on a serving plate and eat at room temperature. Store leftovers in an airtight container in the fridge for up to 3 days.

# Horchata Bibingka

## *Makes 24 bibingka*

Bibingka are Filipino coconut milk–rice cakes baked in banana leaves, and they often contain salted duck egg and cheese. They're a perfect marriage of sweet and savory. I associate bibingka with Christmas because they're a fiesta favorite in my family. Speaking of the holiday season, there's a Vampire Weekend song named after horchata, a drink made from rice soaked in water. In the song, they belt on about drinking it in December, but I digress! I get horchata at Mexican restaurants year-round, and I love its cinnamony flavor. For a sweeter take on bibingka, I like to top the cakes with a horchata glaze. Just make sure to prep the iconic rice drink the night before!

### Horchata

* ½ cup raw long-grain rice (I use jasmine rice because I keep it stocked in my pantry at all times!)
* 1 (3-inch) cinnamon stick
* ½ cup unsweetened, full-fat coconut milk

### Cakes

* 1 (16-ounce) package frozen banana leaves, rinsed and thawed (parchment paper or standard muffin liners can be used as an alternative)
* ¼ cup coconut oil, melted
* 1½ cups rice flour
* ½ cup glutinous rice flour
* 1¾ cups granulated sugar
* 2 teaspoons baking powder
* ¾ teaspoon kosher salt
* 1¼ teaspoons ground cinnamon
* 2 large eggs, at room temperature, lightly whisked
* ¾ cup (1½ sticks) unsalted butter, melted

* 1 (13.5-ounce) can unsweetened, full-fat coconut milk
* 1 teaspoon vanilla extract

### Glaze & Topping

* 1 cup sweetened coconut flakes, for topping
* 2 cups powdered sugar, sifted
* ¼ teaspoon kosher salt
* ½ teaspoon ground cinnamon
* ¼ cup plus 2 tablespoons Horchata
* ¼ teaspoon vanilla extract

### Horchata

1   Place the rice and the cinnamon stick in a small bowl and set aside. Bring 1 cup of water to a boil in a small saucepan and immediately pour it over the contents of the bowl. Cover with a lid and let the mixture sit overnight.

2   The next day, pour the mixture into a blender. Pulse and puree the mixture for

*Continued*

30 seconds until it's smooth. Using a large sieve, strain the liquid from the mixture directly into a small saucepan. Discard any gritty remains that are left in the sieve.

3    Add the coconut milk to the saucepan. Cook over medium-low heat, stirring occasionally with a rubber spatula, until the mixture reduces to about $1/4$ cup plus 2 tablespoons, 8 to 10 minutes.

4    Set the horchata aside and allow it to cool to room temperature.

## Cakes

5    Wipe down the banana leaves and cut them into 24 (5-inch) circles with kitchen scissors. Line two standard cupcake tins with the banana leaf circles. Using a pastry brush, coat the banana leaf-lined tins with the coconut oil.

6    Position an oven rack in the middle of the oven and preheat the oven to 350°F.

7    In a large bowl, mix together the rice flour, glutinous rice flour, granulated sugar, baking powder, salt, and cinnamon with a whisk. Create a large well in the center of the bowl, and then add in the eggs, melted butter, coconut milk, and vanilla. Stirring from the center of the well, whisk the ingredients by hand until the batter is smooth and no streaks of flour remain.

8    Spread the batter evenly among the lined muffin tins, using 3 tablespoons of batter for each cavity. Bake for 20 to 22 minutes, or until a toothpick inserted into the center of a cake comes out clean. Transfer to a wire rack to cool completely.

## Glaze & Topping

9    Place the coconut flakes in a large saucepan. Cook over low heat, stirring occasionally with a wooden spoon, until the coconut flakes are golden brown, 10 to 12 minutes. Set aside.

10    In a medium bowl, whisk together the powdered sugar, salt, ground cinnamon, horchata, and vanilla until the glaze is smooth.

11    Top each bibingka with $1/2$ tablespoon of the horchata glaze and a sprinkle of the toasted coconut flakes. Serve immediately. Store any leftovers in an airtight container at room temperature for up to 3 days.

# Balikbayan

When my parents announced that they were going to bring Argeli and me to the Philippines for a visit in December 2019, I was over the moon. My twenty-four-year-old self was revved up to take some PTO and be a bridesmaid at cousin Ate Kate's wedding. As it was extremely cold coming from the American Northeast, I looked so outlandish wearing a parka at Ninoy Aquino International Airport. It was hot and humid, and the first thing I noticed was that every short man in the crowd could have been my father. I scanned over the heads of weary travelers for a few minutes until I finally found my uncle Alan and the rest of my family with him. We loaded the van with my luggage and proceeded to drive the long two hours from Manila to San Fernando, passing a Jollibee sign every ten miles or so.

It was about 3:30 a.m. by the time we made it to my auntie Aida's house, but she still wanted to give us a warm welcome and feed everyone in sight. I was greeted with hugs and kisses, and a ripe mango to eat with my late-night meal. Both cheeks were cut up for me to effortlessly scoop the fruit with my spoon and shovel it directly into my eager mouth. By the morning, we'd see the rest of my dad's side of the family in droves. My parents set up an assembly line of goodies from the *balikbayan* boxes they brought with them. Balikbayan boxes are cardboard boxes typically packed by Filipinos living abroad to return gifts home to their loved ones in the Philippines. My parents filled their boxes with bags of Lindt chocolate, Hollister T-shirts, and Victoria's Secret lotion to distribute to our relatives.

Seeing my family in Pampanga again after twenty years was such a remarkable experience as a sentient adult. I was taken aback by the familiarity of being around flesh and blood, no matter how many decades had elapsed. When I was five years old, I was too young to fully comprehend the significance of visiting the Philippines for the first time. I remember drinking soda out of plastic bags with a straw and getting mosquito bites the size of golf balls. Lolo Hugo and Lola Undi would give me so many sliced mangoes that all my tank tops were stained orange from the residual juice. At one point during our trip, I jumped into a public pool at the deep end. Since I didn't know how to swim, I almost drowned, but a lifeguard came to save me. It's safe to say that this preliminary trip was merely a collection of disjointed memories. This time, I wanted to know more about my cousins' thoughts on Duterte's presidency, the prominent Christian sects in the Philippines, and just how they were doing now.

While preparing for Ate Kate's big day, we shared so many meals and bounties of fresh tropical fruit together. I was racking up an obscene mango count already, but there was so much more produce I had the good fortune to eat. Besides sweet lakatan bananas and mangosteen, I can't forget trying *kamias* (tree cucumber) for the first time. My dad picked kamias off of Auntie Aida's tree to give to me, and as I took a bite, my lips puckered up

not realizing it would be so sour. Instead of tamarind, you could use kamias as the main flavoring agent in *sinigang*, my favorite Filipino stew. We maximized every day, eating and talking constantly in between dress fittings and dance rehearsals.

In the Philippines, the Christmas season stretches from the months that end in "ber" to January. I arrived after December 25, but we still got to see the Giant Lantern Festival in San Fernando, where humongous parols became the main attraction for elaborate light shows. As the lanterns' colors flashed before my eyes to the tune of Camila Cabello and Shawn Mendes's hit "Señorita," it felt like I was front row at Disneyland's World of Color. All I needed was a warm churro dusted with sugar and cinnamon to bring the experience full circle. When New Year's Eve rolled around, Auntie Aida's house was the party spot for all my relatives to show up with food in hand. On one table, there were the most colorful kakanin as part of the *handaan*. The oodles and oodles of purple, orange, and amber rice cakes were cut up into squares and laid out on a banana leaf-lined platter. The sheer abundance was already a feast for the eyes, but sinking my teeth into each chewy dessert took me to cloud nine. I felt so, so lucky to ring in the new year and share kakanin with them. I knew hours of work went into mixing, steaming, and toasting coconut curds for the kakanin, which made it all the more special to me.

In our last week and a half in the motherland, we squeezed in a plethora of sightseeing. We

drove up to my mom's hometown, Santa Ana. We took plenty of photos outside of where her childhood house used to be, which was now a bookstore and a butcher shop. My parents, Argeli, and I took a flight to Palawan to check out the phenomenal Puerto Princesa Underground River by boat. With my uncle Noel and auntie Reggie, we were able to tour the Taal volcano island on horseback. No more than a couple days after we visited, the volcano erupted for the first time in forty-three years, and it spewed so much ash around Manila that we weren't sure if we'd be able to fly home.

It was a whirlwind trip that ended with the beautiful nuptials of Ate Kate and her new husband, Daryl. I cried when I saw her walk down the aisle, and it was just touching to see this big moment in real life, not through photos on Instagram or a Facebook post. It was hard to part ways the next day because we had all gotten so close again. Before loading the van for the airport, Argeli refused to get inside. She was also sad to leave. When every single one of our relatives patiently pretended to join us in the van as a way to coax her inside, I choked up. I wish our time together never had to end. Once we made it to the airport, my parents and Argeli had to board the first of a series of connecting flights to California as I waited for mine to New York. Even before the pandemic, the reality of living in a diaspora was the uncertainty of when you'd see your family again. That feeling overwhelmed me as I made my long solo journey back to America, not knowing what the rest of 2020 had in store for us all.

# Cookies & Cream Suman Moron

*Makes 16 suman*

There is a massive assortment of suman, sticky and chewy rice cakes steamed in banana leaves, of varying flavors, shapes, and sizes across the Philippines. Every region has its specialties, and you could write a whole book on suman alone. My favorite is a specialty from Eastern Visayas, suman moron, which consists of a swirl of plain and chocolate glutinous rice flour dough. It feels like you're opening a present whenever you're unwrapping suman, and suman moron is no exception. Each one you unravel from its leaf wrapper is a stunning culinary gift.

Growing up, I would microwave milk and crushed-up Oreos to eat like a pudding. Before TikTok made it a thing, I thought I was a genius. The addition of literal Oreos, cream centers and all, in the suman moron dough is my new take on this old hack of mine. Whenever I take a bite of this dessert, I feel like the novelty hasn't worn off in the slightest.

* 1 (16-ounce) package frozen banana leaves, rinsed and thawed (parchment paper can be used as an alternative)
* 4 Oreo sandwich cookies
* 1 cup glutinous rice flour
* ½ cup rice flour
* 1½ cups unsweetened, full-fat coconut milk
* ½ cup granulated sugar
* ½ teaspoon kosher salt
* ½ cup packed dark brown sugar
* 2 tablespoons unsweetened cocoa powder
* ¼ cup coconut oil, melted

1   Wipe down the banana leaves. Using kitchen scissors, cut each banana leaf into rectangles 7 inches wide and 10 inches long. Repeat until you have 16 rectangles. Reserve 32 banana leaf strips or use kitchen twine for tying the suman later. Set aside.

2   Take each Oreo and twist open the cookie halves. Scrape the cream filling into a small bowl. Place the cookie parts in a food processor and blitz for 5 to 8 pulses, until the cookies are finely ground. You should have ¼ cup of cookie crumbs.

3   In a large saucepan, combine the cream filling, ½ cup of the glutinous rice flour, ¼ cup of the rice flour, ¾ cup of the coconut milk, the granulated sugar, and salt. Cook over low heat, stirring frequently with a rubber spatula, until the mixture forms a dough, 5 to 7 minutes. To test if it's done,

*Continued*

poke the dough; nothing should stick to your finger. Transfer the dough to a small bowl and cover it with a paper towel moistened with water so that it doesn't dry out. Set aside.

4    Using the same saucepan, combine the cookie crumbs, the remaining $1/2$ cup glutinous rice flour, the remaining $1/4$ cup rice flour, the remaining $3/4$ cup coconut milk, the brown sugar, and cocoa powder. Repeat the cooking process from the previous step. Transfer the chocolate dough to a small bowl and cover it with a paper towel moistened with water so that it doesn't dry out.

5    Prepare a steamer by filling a large pot with 2 inches of water and fitting the pot with a steel steaming rack. Bring the water to a boil over medium-high heat.

6    Take one banana leaf rectangle and, using a pastry brush, grease one side with the coconut oil. Scoop 1 tablespoon of each type of dough and roll into logs that are $4^{1}/2$ inches long. Place the logs side by side in the center of the rectangle. Starting from one side, stick the ends of the logs together and proceed to twist over each other twice, creating a swirl. Stick the opposite ends together to seal the swirled dough. Picking up the long ends of the banana leaf, roll the twisted log in a back-and-forth motion until the log is $5^{1}/2$ inches long.

7    Roll up the suman in the banana leaf and then proceed to twist and tightly tie each end with one of the reserved strips. Repeat the process with the rest of the doughs until you have 16 suman.

8    Place the suman on the steaming rack and cover the pot with a lid. Depending on the size of your steamer, you may have to steam the suman in multiple batches and add more water as you go. Steam the suman until firm, 25 to 30 minutes. Using tongs, remove the suman and place on a tray. Serve warm. Store any leftovers in an airtight container in the fridge for up to 3 days.

# Speculoos Biko

*Makes 12 servings*

If I'm flying Delta, there's a 99 percent chance that I'm asking for the Biscoff cookies as my snack of choice. These speculoos cookies from Belgium have a deep molasses flavor reminiscent of gingerbread. Once speculoos cookie butter spread made its way Stateside via Trader Joe's, I was hooked. I remember telling everyone I knew in 2016 to get themselves a jar. For this biko recipe, I couldn't resist adding cookie butter to the sticky rice. It makes for an even creamier biko both inside the cake and as a topping (complete with a sprinkle of latik!). Biko is a decadent rice cake traditionally made with glutinous rice, brown sugar, and coconut milk. It's another dessert staple when my family gets together for special occasions. While soaking the rice overnight can be a test of your patience, this step helps quicken the cooking process the next day.

* 2 cups uncooked glutinous rice
* I frozen banana leaf, rinsed and thawed (parchment paper can be used as an alternative)
* I tablespoon coconut oil, melted
* I (13.5-ounce) can unsweetened, full-fat coconut milk
* I cup packed dark brown sugar
* ³/₄ cup plus 2 tablespoons speculoos cookie butter
* ¹/₂ teaspoon kosher salt
* I tablespoon Latik (page 30)

1  The night before serving, in a medium bowl, rinse the glutinous rice with cold water until the water runs clear. Using a large sieve, drain the water from the rice and place the rice back in the bowl. Add enough fresh water to completely cover the rice and cover the bowl with a lid. Let the rice sit overnight at room temperature. After the rice is done soaking, drain the rice using a large sieve. Set aside.

2  Wipe down the banana leaf and line an 8 × 8-inch square pan with it, making sure you have I to 2 inches of overhang on all sides. You can cut any excess with kitchen scissors. Using a pastry brush, grease the lined pan with the coconut oil. Set aside.

3  Combine 2¹/₂ cups water, the coconut milk, brown sugar, ¹/₂ cup of the cookie butter, and

*Continued*

salt in a large saucepan. Cook over medium-high heat, stirring occasionally with a rubber spatula, until the mixture comes to a boil, 11 to 12 minutes. Once it starts boiling, immediately stir in the rice. Reduce the heat to low. Simmer, stirring frequently, until the mixture is thick and the rice has absorbed the liquid, 15 to 17 minutes.

4   Transfer the rice to the prepared baking pan and spread it evenly with the rubber spatula.

5   Spread the remaining $1/4$ cup plus 2 tablespoons cookie butter over the top of the rice. Let the biko cool for 15 minutes before cutting into diamonds or squares and sprinkle each serving with $1/4$ teaspoon of the latik. Store leftovers in an airtight container in the fridge for up to 4 days.

# Pandan & Anise Puto

*Makes 48 puto*

Puto is a staple for any handaan, or feast. These steamed rice cakes are meant to be laden onto a full plate, so you can eat them alongside your ulam, or main dish. I even love adding puto to a helping of pancit, or Filipino stir-fried noodles. There are many variations of puto, ranging from some topped with cheese and others made with ube. In college, my ading Carissa's mom even brought us her specialty: puto pao, which is puto stuffed with a savory pork filling. My recipe leans on the sweet side with pandan as the star, but the licorice-like anise seeds help to cleanse the palate between bites of ulam. I enjoy eating this puto to accompany a larger meal, but it's delightful to eat these as standalone desserts too.

* I frozen pandan leaf (optional, but it is ideal to use if you want more of an intense flavor instead of just using the extract alone), thawed and tied into a knot
* Nonstick spray
* $3/4$ cup unsweetened, full-fat coconut milk
* I large egg white, at room temperature
* $1/4$ teaspoon pandan extract
* I cup rice flour
* I tablespoon baking powder
* $1/4$ cup plus 2 tablespoons sugar
* $1/4$ teaspoon kosher salt
* $1/4$ teaspoon plus a pinch anise seeds

1   In a small saucepan, bring $1/4$ cup water to a boil and then add in the pandan knot, if using. Turn off the heat and let the pandan knot steep in the water for 10 minutes. Remove the pandan knot and set the water aside.

2   Spray 48 mini muffin molds with nonstick spray and set aside. I like to use silicone molds for steaming these cakes because the aluminum pans tend to be too big for my steamer.

3   In a large measuring cup, whisk together the pandan-infused water, if using the pandan leaf (if not, use $1/4$ cup regular water), coconut milk, egg white, and pandan extract until well combined.

4   In a medium bowl, whisk together the rice flour, baking powder, sugar, and salt until the baking powder is evenly distributed.

5   Pour the wet ingredients into the bowl. Whisk until the batter is smooth. Let the batter rest uncovered until some tiny bubbles form at

*Continued*

the surface, 5 to 7 minutes. This resting time allows for the flour to better absorb the liquid and helps the puto rise better. While the batter is resting, prepare a steamer by filling a large pot with 2 inches of water and fitting the pot with a steel steaming rack. Bring the water to a boil over medium-high heat.

6   Fill each muffin cavity with I tablespoon of the batter. Sprinkle a couple of the anise seeds on top of each one.

7   Place the molds on the steaming rack and cover the pot with a lid. Depending on the size of your steamer, you may have to steam the puto in multiple batches and add more water as you go. Steam for 7 to 8 minutes, or until a toothpick inserted in one comes out clean. When you gently touch the tops of the puto they should spring back. Be careful not to burn yourself while testing them for doneness.

8   Using tongs, remove the molds from the steamer and allow the puto to cool for I minute before inverting them onto a plate. Repeat this process until all the puto are cooked.

9   Serve the puto once they've cooled to room temperature. Store any leftovers in an airtight container in the fridge for up to 3 days.

# Thai Tea Kutsinta

*Makes 14 kutsinta*

Of all the different types of kakanin, I gravitate toward kutsinta the most because I love me a handheld, chewy dessert. The molasses in the brown sugar is the predominant flavor of traditional kutsinta, which are steamed in aluminum egg tart molds. It feels like you're eating a larger-than-average cold tapioca pearl disc topped with grated coconut. When I first visited Johnny Air Mart, a Filipino food market in the East Village, I was ecstatic that they were selling ready-made kutsinta in their refrigerated section. As a kid, I was so used to only having them for New Year's or Christmas, so it felt like quite a treat to find it in the wild.

While annatto seeds typically give kutsinta their orange hue, I use Thai tea instead for a distinctive color and flavor. When I came up with the idea of pairing Thai tea with this recipe, I was thinking of Thai tea blondies that I had baked months before. The tea's spices complemented the brown sugar in the blondies, so I thought it would go well with kutsinta too. Thai tea, with its base of brewed black tea, is creamy and sweet and has warm undertones of star anise, cardamom, and cloves. If you want to go the extra mile for these Thai tea kutsinta, all you're missing is a drizzle of condensed milk.

* I teaspoon Thai tea mix
* 1/4 cup tapioca starch
* 1/4 cup glutinous rice flour
* 1/2 cup all-purpose flour
* 3/4 cup packed dark brown sugar
* I teaspoon lye water (see page 14)
* Nonstick spray
* I cup fresh grated coconut, for topping
* Sweetened condensed milk, for topping (optional)

1 In a small saucepan, bring 1½ cups water to a boil. Once it's boiling, stir in the Thai tea mix using a wooden spoon. Turn off the heat, and let the tea steep for 10 minutes. While the tea is steeping, prepare a steamer by filling a large pot with 2 inches of water and fitting the pot with a steel steaming rack. Bring the water to a boil over medium-high heat.

2 Using a large sieve, strain the tea into a medium bowl. Discard the used tea leaves. Whisk in the tapioca starch, glutinous rice flour, all-purpose flour, brown sugar, and lye water.

3 Spray 14 aluminum egg tart molds with nonstick spray. Pour 3 tablespoons of the batter in each mold.

*Continued*

4   Place the molds on the steaming rack and cover the pot with a lid. Depending on the size of your steamer, you may have to steam the kutsinta in multiple batches and add more water as you go. Steam for 25 to 30 minutes, or until the kutsinta are set. Remove the molds from the steamer and let them cool at room temperature for 15 minutes before transferring to the fridge. Chill for at least 2 hours.

5   Once the kutsinta are cold, use a small rubber spatula to gently loosen them from their molds. Place them on a plate and then top each with a generous amount of the fresh grated coconut. Drizzle with condensed milk, if desired. Store any leftovers in an airtight container in the fridge for up to 3 days.

# Marbled Tahini Palitaw

*Makes 37 palitaw*

Palitaw are chewy glutinous rice cakes that get a burst of flavor from toppings of coconut, sesame, and sugar. My mom is a big fan of palitaw as a snack because she likes that they're not overly sweet and she spends little to no time in the kitchen making them. *Litaw* literally means "to float," which is what the rice cakes do when they're done boiling. While you essentially only need glutinous rice flour and water to make palitaw, I wanted to integrate sesame into the dough itself by adding tahini. Not only are the palitaw more flavorful, but using two types of tahini makes them two-toned.

* I¹/₄ cups glutinous rice flour
* I¹/₂ tablespoons plain tahini
* I¹/₂ tablespoons black tahini
* I cup unsweetened shredded coconut
* ¹/₂ cup sugar
* 2 tablespoons tuxedo sesame seeds, toasted

1  In a small bowl, combine the glutinous rice flour and ¹/₂ cup water. Using your hands, knead the ingredients together until the mixture turns into a pliable dough.

2  Divide the dough in half and place each half in a medium bowl.

3  Add the plain tahini to one of the bowls and knead the dough together until well combined. Split the dough into two balls.

4  Add the black tahini to the other bowl and knead the dough together until well combined. Split the dough into two balls.

5  Place one of the black tahini dough balls on a work surface and flatten to about ¹/₂ inch thick with your palm. Place a plain tahini dough ball on top of the flattened dough and flatten it to the same size. Repeat with the other two balls, making sure to alternate the colors.

6  Lightly knead the stack of dough until the dough colors are marbled, being careful not to

*Continued*

over-knead because the colors will muddle and turn into one gray mass.

7   Once the dough is marbled, use a rolling pin to roll it out $1/4$ inch thick. Using a $1^1/_2$-inch round cookie cutter, cut out circles of the dough and place them on a plate. Gather and reroll the scraps until you've cut out as many circles as you can.

8   Fill a medium saucepan with water and bring to a boil over medium-high heat.

9   Drop 10 to 12 dough circles into the boiling water and gently stir so that none of them stick to the bottom. Boil until the circles rise and float to the top, 50 to 60 seconds. Immediately scoop them out with a wire mesh skimmer and place them on a plate.

10   Coat the cooked palitaw in coconut. Serve them warm or at room temperature on a plate with a sprinkle of the sugar and toasted sesame seeds. Since the palitaw harden if chilled, they are best enjoyed right away.

# Espasol Bites

*Makes 34 bites*

Espasol is a type of kakanin from the province of Laguna in the Philippines. The primary ingredients of espasol are toasted rice flour, coconut milk, and sugar. They're usually shaped in the form of mochi-like logs, but I opt for tinier bites with my recipe so they're not as messy to pick up and eat. Whenever I would pick up a cylinder of traditional espasol, I'd get my clothes covered in the rice flour coating.

Another big change is that I use panela, which is a Latin American unrefined cane sugar. It's also known as piloncillo or chancaca. You might find panela in hard cone or disc shapes, but you can grate it to use in your desserts. Panela has a complex flavor that reminds me of a deep, dark caramel with some smoky undertones. If your local grocery store doesn't carry panela, you can use dark brown sugar for this recipe.

* ½ cup plus 2 tablespoons glutinous rice flour
* ¾ cup unsweetened, full-fat coconut milk
* ½ cup grated panela
* ½ teaspoon vanilla extract
* ¼ teaspoon kosher salt

1   Place the glutinous rice flour in a large saucepan. Cook over low heat, stirring occasionally with a wooden spoon, until lightly browned and fragrant, 12 to 15 minutes. Remove from the heat.

2   Place ¼ cup of the toasted flour in a small bowl. Leave the remainder in the large saucepan.

3   Add the coconut milk, grated panela, vanilla, and salt to the large saucepan. Cook the mixture over low heat, stirring frequently with a wooden spoon, until it forms a sticky dough, 10 to 12 minutes. The flour should be evenly incorporated in the mixture.

4   Lightly flour a rolling pin and your work surface with the reserved toasted glutinous rice flour. Place the espasol dough on the work surface and roll out about ½ inch thick.

5   Using a mini flower-shaped cookie cutter, cut out espasol flower bites. Roll in excess flour and place on a plate. Alternatively, you can just cut the dough into ½-inch cubes if you don't have cookie cutters.

6   Serve immediately and store any leftovers in an airtight container at room temperature for up to 3 days.

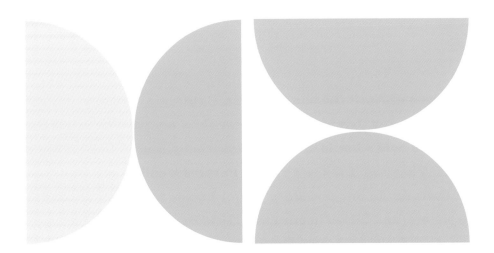

# PART II
## San Jose, California

*Everywhere You Look*

**I was born in April 1995, in San Jose, California. Prone to tantrums and impatiently drinking milk faster than my parents could teach me how to hold a bottle, I was an Aries baby, and an extra-fiery one at that. They say it takes a village to raise a child—my family took that literally. In our one-story rental house, my mom, my dad, my two sisters, and I lived in one room; Lolo Benjie and two uncles were in another room; and then Auntie Rina, Uncle Che, and two cousins, Ate Dinah and Ate Iris, were in the last room. We were living our own Filipino version of *Full House*. In this multigenerational home with a giant persimmon tree in the backyard, I was nurtured by so many people of all ages who loved me.**

**I** *didn't know at the time* how much real estate was in the Bay Area, and I knew even less that we lived together with such little space out of necessity. Even though my parents were both working full-time, one of my relatives would still walk me home from kindergarten every day. When I was younger, I remember when I first tried speaking Kapampangan words and my parents laughed at my American accent. It dissuaded me from learning how to talk in Kapampangan at all then. I could still translate what my family said, but I didn't know how to carry a conversation. For some time,

I wondered how many of our conflicts were due to a language barrier and just a series of miscommunication.

Even within a big family that loved one another dearly, I sometimes clashed with my parents when they wouldn't give me an explanation for their decisions. Both my parents are devout Catholics, and they made it a point to take us to mass every Sunday morning. As a rebellious kid, I'd question the necessity of going all the time. I'd pretend to be asleep in order to avoid getting up early. However, I was easily bribed by the promise of McDonald's hotcakes for breakfast after going to church. Who could say no to a stack of sweet pancakes dripping in sticky, artificial maple syrup? Whenever I'd do something even slightly out of pocket, my parents would caution me against acting out so I wouldn't end up in hell one day. Harsh words to hear for a small child! I asked them "Why?" to little to no avail. At most, each would tell me a version of "Because I said so." Today, I believe much of my willingness to challenge the conventions of traditional desserts was derived from this insatiable curiosity.

My younger sister, Argeli, was diagnosed with severe nonverbal autism when she was a baby. My parents struggled with days when she'd bang her head against the wall and couldn't tell us what was bothering her. Instead of sitting down with Ginelle and me to talk through the challenges they faced, my parents didn't utter a word. I felt like they brushed a lot of issues under the rug, and in hindsight, they probably wanted to shield us from their pain. I knew it was difficult for them, and that our extended family wanted to help as much as they could. Sometimes, my uncle Jones would drive Ginelle and me to our local Dollar Tree for a shopping spree in the candy aisle. He was our fun uncle who spoiled us to pieces. I would come home with bags of Warheads that were so sour, I sometimes had to rinse the hard candy's top layer of citric acid with water before popping another one in my sore mouth. I've always had a sweet tooth, which is directly correlated to the astronomical number of cavities I've gotten in my lifetime.

Besides having lots of family members in our house, we also had relatives back in the Philippines to talk to using calling cards. Back in the early 2000s, you had to pay to dial long-distance numbers. Whenever I'd wake up and hear my relatives exchanging gossip early in the morning, I'd let the comforting sound of their voices wash over me like a wave. Ate Dinah worked at the local Goldilocks, the famous Filipino bakery chain, and she got me my dream Winnie-the-Pooh birthday cake. I still remember it so vividly because my eyes widened seeing the plastic balloons and royal icing flowers on top of it. When I think of San Jose, I always think of it as a place of celebration. Every summer, my cousins Anna, JB, Ate Charm, and Christopher would all come from Jersey and Chino Hills for our mini reunions. That usually meant karaoke and long feasts at Auntie Flor's house, where we would eat Filipino fare like Valerio's pancit palabok and sizzling *sisig*.

Although we eventually moved to Stockton, my parents couldn't keep us away from the 408. We'd make excuses to drive an hour to see a newly born niece or nephew, or to go to our family dentist still based in Berryessa. Whenever we'd stop at a store or run an errand, it was inevitable that my dad would run into a stranger and start speaking in Tagalog with them. I'd ask him, "How did you know they were Filipino too?" And he'd succinctly reply, "You can just tell." I'd question him further and he wouldn't say much else, but I get it more now as I've gotten older. The longer you go on, the smaller the world gets.

# CAKES

Cakes are the centerpieces of celebration for birthdays, weddings, and life-changing events. Sometimes, the cakes that you have for a school snack or to munch on casually can be just as memorable.

# Mini Salabundt Cakes

### *Makes 26 mini cakes*

Salabat is a Filipino tea that you make by steeping ginger in boiling water. When I visited the Philippines in the winter of 2019, I got a cold adjusting to the drastic temperature difference between chilly New York and the hot and humid tropics. My mom immediately started making salabat for me when she heard me cough. Since I have a sweet tooth, I added copious amounts of lemon and honey to my mug. It's a soothing concoction when you have an itchy throat, and I always associate it with how my parents would take care of me when I was younger (and even now, when I'm in my twenties).

I came up with salabundt cakes after rewatching *My Big Fat Greek Wedding*, and then seeing the scene in the movie where Toula's Greek mother balks at a gifted Bundt cake. Her puzzlement about a cake with a hole in it is a master class in comedy, and made me think lovingly of my own mom. Inspired by the salabat my mother would brew for me, these mini salabundt cakes taste like moist gingerbread, and the batter includes both fresh and ground ginger. Fresh ginger makes a huge difference you can taste, and I recommend taking the time to grate it. There are also candied ginger bits adorning the glaze.

## Cake

* Nonstick baking spray with flour
* $2^1/_2$ cups all-purpose flour
* I cup packed dark brown sugar
* $^1/_2$ teaspoon kosher salt
* $1^3/_4$ teaspoons baking soda
* $^3/_4$ teaspoon baking powder
* $^3/_4$ teaspoon ground cinnamon
* $1^1/_2$ teaspoons ground ginger
* $^1/_4$ teaspoon ground nutmeg
* $^1/_4$ teaspoon ground cloves
* 2 large eggs, at room temperature, lightly whisked
* $^3/_4$ cup robust molasses
* 2 tablespoons fresh grated ginger
* I cup buttermilk, at room temperature
* $^1/_2$ cup vegetable oil
* I teaspoon vanilla extract

## Glaze

* 3 cups powdered sugar, sifted
* Zest of I lemon
* $^1/_4$ teaspoon vanilla extract
* 3 tablespoons honey
* $^1/_4$ cup plus I tablespoon fresh lemon juice
* Candied ginger, finely diced

## Cake

1   Position a rack in the middle of the oven and preheat the oven to 350°F. Grease the cavities of 26 mini muffin-style Bundt cake pans with nonstick baking spray. I like the baking spray that has flour already in it because it helps cakes without paper liners release easily.

2   Whisk the flour, dark brown sugar, salt, baking soda, baking powder, cinnamon, ground ginger, nutmeg, and cloves in a large bowl until well combined. Create a large well in the center of the mixture, and then add in the eggs, molasses, fresh grated ginger, buttermilk, oil, and vanilla. Stirring from the center of the well, whisk the ingredients by hand until the batter is smooth and there are no visible streaks of flour. Fill each prepared mini Bundt cake cavity with 3 tablespoons of the batter.

3   Bake one pan at a time for 10 to 12 minutes, or until a toothpick inserted into the center of one cake comes out clean. Transfer the pan to a wire rack to cool for 5 minutes. Repeat the process with the other pan until all your mini Bundt cakes are baked.

4   Loosen the edges of each cake with a small rubber spatula. Then place a baking sheet over one pan and turn over the pan and baking sheet together to invert the cakes. Place the unmolded cakes on the wire rack to cool completely. Repeat the process with the other pan.

## Glaze

5   In a medium bowl, combine the powdered sugar, lemon zest, and vanilla.

6   Place the honey and lemon juice in a small microwave-safe bowl, and microwave for 30 seconds. Pour the hot mixture into the sugar mixture, then whisk until the mixture turns into a thick white glaze.

7   Using a piping bag fitted with a small round tip, pipe glaze onto the mini Bundt cakes and top with bits of diced candied ginger. Let the glaze harden for 30 minutes before serving at room temperature. Store leftovers at room temperature in an airtight container for up to 4 days.

# Confetti Pianono

## *Makes 8 servings*

I'm a sucker for birthday cake–flavored anything. I gobble up Coldstone's Birthday Cake Remix, buy Glossier's Birthday Balm Dotcom, and I especially love Milk Bar's colorful Birthday Cake. This Filipino roll cake recipe draws heavy inspiration from that celebration cake in particular. Although a traditional pianono is made up of a vanilla- or ube-flavored sponge cake filled with butter and sugar, you can draw up a bevy of cake and filling combinations for pianonos. With the addition of sprinkles and imitation vanilla extract to the batter, a light whipped cream filling, and a sweet buttercream frosting dotted with nonpareils galore, all these colorful elements and flavors bring out the rainbow motif of my pianono. Fun fact: The pianono cake was originally named after Pope Pius IX!

## Cake

- ❋ Nonstick spray
- ❋ I cup plus 2 tablespoons cake flour
- ❋ 1½ teaspoons baking powder
- ❋ ¼ teaspoon kosher salt
- ❋ 4 large eggs, at room temperature
- ❋ ⅓ cup whole milk, at room temperature
- ❋ ¾ teaspoon clear imitation vanilla extract
- ❋ ¼ cup vegetable oil
- ❋ ¾ cup granulated sugar
- ❋ ½ cup rainbow jimmies
- ❋ ½ teaspoon cream of tartar
- ❋ ¼ cup powdered sugar

## Whipped Cream Filling

- ❋ 1½ cups heavy cream, cold
- ❋ ¼ cup plus 2 tablespoons powdered sugar
- ❋ ¾ teaspoon clear imitation vanilla extract

## Buttercream Frosting

- ❋ 8 tablespoons (I stick) unsalted butter, at room temperature
- ❋ 1½ cups powdered sugar, sifted
- ❋ ½ teaspoon kosher salt
- ❋ I teaspoon clear imitation vanilla extract
- ❋ 2 tablespoons heavy cream
- ❋ Rainbow nonpareils or sprinkles, for decoration

## Cake

1   Position a rack in the middle of the oven and preheat the oven to 325°F. Grease a 10 × 15-inch jelly roll pan with nonstick spray and line with parchment paper and set aside.

2   In a small bowl, mix together the cake flour, baking powder, and salt until the baking powder is evenly distributed. Set aside.

*Continued*

3   Separate the eggs, placing the yolks in a large bowl and the egg whites in a clean and dry medium bowl.

4   In the large bowl, whisk the egg yolks, milk, imitation vanilla, oil, and ¼ cup of the granulated sugar by hand. Slowly add in the flour mixture and continue to whisk until well combined. Using a rubber spatula, fold in the rainbow jimmies until evenly distributed in the batter.

5   In the medium bowl, beat the egg whites and cream of tartar with an electric hand mixer on medium-high speed until soft peaks form, 1 to 2 minutes. Gradually add in the remaining ½ cup granulated sugar and beat until stiff peaks form, another 1 to 2 minutes.

6   Using a rubber spatula, gently fold the meringue into the flour mixture in three batches until fully incorporated into the batter. Pour the batter into the prepared jelly roll pan. Dust a 20 × 30-inch kitchen towel with the powdered sugar and set aside.

7   Bake the cake for 14 to 16 minutes, or until a toothpick inserted into the center comes out clean and the top of the cake is lightly browned.

8   Take the pan out of the oven and immediately turn over onto the prepared kitchen towel. Peel off the parchment paper and discard. Starting from the narrow end, roll the warm cake embedded in the kitchen towel and let it cool at room temperature for 30 minutes, seam side down.

9   While the roll is still in the towel, transfer it to the fridge to cool for 1 hour.

## Whipped Cream Filling

10   In a medium bowl, beat the heavy cream, powdered sugar, and imitation vanilla with an electric hand mixer on medium-high speed until stiff peaks form, 3 to 4 minutes.

11   Cover the bowl with plastic wrap and store in the fridge until you're ready to assemble the cake.

## Buttercream Frosting

12   Place the butter and powdered sugar in the bowl of a stand mixer fitted with the paddle attachment. Cream on medium-high speed for 2 to 3 minutes, until light and fluffy.

13   Gradually stir in the salt, imitation vanilla, and heavy cream and beat for 1 minute. Scrape down the bowl and sides with a rubber spatula and beat for another minute, or until well combined. Set aside.

## Assembly

14   Take the cake out of the fridge and unroll. Spread the whipped cream evenly over the surface of the cake, leaving a 1-inch margin on one of the short ends.

15   Starting at the short end covered in cream, tightly roll the cake into a log shape. Wrap the cake log back in the towel and twist the ends to seal. Return the cake to the fridge to chill for 2 hours to set, seam side down.

16   After 2 hours, remove the cake from the fridge and cover with an even layer of the buttercream frosting. Coat in rainbow nonpareils on all sides of the cake. Serve cold on a rectangular plate. Store any leftovers in an airtight container in the fridge for up to 4 days.

# Pineapple Upside-Down Guava Cupcakes

*Makes 14 cupcakes*

When I think of pineapple upside-down cake, my mind goes straight to images of *I Love Lucy* and old-school Coca-Cola commercials. Pineapple upside-down cake is the American retro-chic answer to tarte tatin. With a surface of shiny maraschino cherries and pineapple rings drenched in brown sugar syrup, the dessert is Norman Rockwell–esque and fit for any special occasion. It's beautiful in the simplicity of its presentation, but I wanted to make the cake into individual sizes for easy distribution among family and friends. One of my least favorite tasks at a party is to cut a whole cake. My hands always shake because I struggle with getting even slices. Turning this into a cupcake recipe relieves me of all cake-cutting duties.

My version also adds one more tropical flavor to the mix: guava. I wanted to bring new life to the traditional vanilla cake base, and I love how guava stands up to the pineapple. Ripe guava has a unique flavor that can be likened to a mix of strawberry, pear, and mango. Reducing guava nectar into a thick syrup and mixing it into the batter allows it to permeate the finished cake with its flavor. Not to mention, the cake itself just looks prettier when it's pink!

* I (33.8-ounce) carton guava nectar
* Nonstick baking spray with flour
* ½ pound (2 sticks) unsalted butter
* 2 cups packed dark brown sugar
* 2 (20-ounce) cans pineapple slices in 100% pineapple juice
* 14 maraschino cherries without stems
* 2½ cups all-purpose flour
* ½ teaspoon kosher salt
* I cup granulated sugar
* I teaspoon baking soda
* ¾ teaspoon baking powder
* 2 large eggs, at room temperature, lightly whisked

* I cup buttermilk, at room temperature
* ½ cup vegetable oil
* I teaspoon vanilla extract
* 2 to 3 drops red gel food coloring

1   Pour the guava nectar into a medium saucepan. Cook over medium-low heat, stirring occasionally using a rubber spatula, until the nectar has reduced to ³/₄ cup, 38 to 40 minutes. Turn off the heat. Transfer the reduced nectar to a small bowl and let cool at room temperature.

*Continued*

2   Position a rack in the middle of the oven and preheat the oven to 350°F.

3   Grease 14 cavities of jumbo muffin pans with nonstick baking spray. Trace the bottom of a muffin cup, cut 14 circles of matching diameter out of parchment paper, and line the cavities with these circles.

4   In a small saucepan, combine the butter and brown sugar. Cook over medium-high heat, stirring occasionally with a rubber spatula, until the butter is melted, 2 to 3 minutes. Pour 1 tablespoon of the mixture into each lined muffin cavity.

5   Using a large sieve, drain the pineapple slices and discard the juice (or save it to drink). There should be a total of 20 slices, but you will only need 14 for this recipe. Place one pineapple slice in each cavity. Place a maraschino cherry in the middle of each slice.

6   Whisk the all-purpose flour, salt, granulated sugar, baking soda, and baking powder in a large bowl. Create a large well in the center of the mixture, and then add in the reduced guava nectar, eggs, buttermilk, oil, vanilla, and red gel food coloring. Stirring from the center of the well, whisk the ingredients by hand until the batter is smooth and there are no visible streaks of flour. Fill each jumbo muffin cavity with $1/3$ cup of batter.

7   Bake for 17 to 20 minutes, or until a toothpick inserted into the center of one cupcake comes out clean. Transfer the pans to a wire rack and let cool for 5 minutes.

8   Place a baking sheet over each muffin pan, and turn over the muffin pan and baking sheet together to invert the cakes. Discard the parchment paper circles. Serve warm. Store any leftovers in an airtight container in the fridge for up to 4 days.

# Ube Macapuno Molten Lava Cakes

*Makes 2 servings*

Jon Favreau's character in *Chef* had a meltdown over molten choclate lava cakes, but I swear making them doesn't have to be a stressful experience! As long as you don't overbake them, you'll be able to achieve those ooey-gooey centers. Classic ube macapuno cake—with its layers of ube chiffon, buttercream, and sweet coconut sport strings—is near and dear to my heart. Seeing any variation of this cake takes me back to being five years old, and gazing longingly at it in the window of our local Goldilocks. There were so many desserts at this Filipino bakery chain that I wanted to take home with me, but I just adored this cake so much.

For ube macapuno molten lava cakes, mixing in ube halaya with white chocolate adds that iconic flavor to the batter. Once these tiny cakes are out of the oven and served with a dollop of macapuno and whipped cream, you're ready to impress a date or even the most curmudgeonly of restaurant critics.

* Nonstick baking spray with flour
* 8 tablespoons (I stick) unsalted butter
* ³⁄₄ cup white chocolate chips
* 2 tablespoons ube halaya, store-bought or homemade (page 24)
* 2 tablespoons powdered sugar, plus more for dusting
* ¹⁄₂ teaspoon ube extract
* I large egg plus I large egg yolk, at room temperature
* ¹⁄₂ cup all-purpose flour
* ¹⁄₂ teaspoon kosher salt
* 2 tablespoons macapuno strings
* Canned whipped cream
* 2 maraschino cherries with stems

1   Position a rack in the middle of the oven and preheat the oven to 425°F. Grease two 6-ounce ramekins with nonstick baking spray and set aside.

2   Combine the butter and white chocolate chips in a medium microwave-safe bowl. Microwave for 30-second intervals and stir the mixture between each round until the chocolate has melted completely.

3   Whisk in the ube halaya, powdered sugar, ube extract, egg, and egg yolk until well combined. Stir in the all-purpose flour and the salt. Mix until there are no visible flour streaks.

4   Divide the cake batter evenly between the prepared ramekins. Place the ramekins onto a baking sheet and bake for II to I4 minutes, or until

*Continued*

the sides of the cakes are solid but the centers are somewhat soft when the ramekins are slightly jiggled.

5    Let the ramekins cool on the baking tray for I minute, then cover each with a small serving plate and immediately turn over to release the cake onto the plate.

6    Dust with powdered sugar using a small sieve, top each with I tablespoon of the macapuno strings, then garnish each with whipped cream and a cherry on top. Serve warm.

# Lychee Madeleines with Hibiscus Tea Glaze & Dried Rose Petals

*Makes 26 madeleines*

Madeleines are shell-shaped sponge cakes that taste fantastic with a dose of lychee flavor. Besides lychee extract in the batter, there is hibiscus tea–steeped lychee juice in the glaze. Topping the madeleines with dried rose petals really accentuates the fruit's floral notes. I baked these for the first time in April 2021 for a collaboration dessert box with my friends at Bowl Cut Table, a cooking and baking collective based in New York. Since we were doing a spring-themed box, I wanted to contribute a dessert that was light, fruity, and featured some type of flower to go with a season of everything in bloom.

They were such a huge success that I have done countless batches since then. I was honored that my friend Reenie even asked me to make 150 of these for her wedding. You don't need an occasion to whip up lychee madeleines, but they are showstoppers on any dessert table.

* 10 tablespoons (1 stick plus 2 tablespoons) unsalted butter
* 1 cup all-purpose flour
* 1/2 teaspoon baking powder
* 1/8 teaspoon kosher salt
* 3 large eggs, at room temperature
* 2/3 cup granulated sugar
* 1 tablespoon lychee extract
* 1/4 cup lychee juice
* 1 hibiscus tea bag
* 1 1/2 cups powdered sugar, sifted
* Dried rose petals, for garnish

1   Place 1 stick of the butter in a medium saucepan over medium-low heat. Stir occasionally with a rubber spatula as the butter melts and continue to cook until it gets golden brown, 5 to 7 minutes. Pour the browned butter into a medium bowl and let cool slightly.

2   In a small bowl, whisk together the all-purpose flour, baking powder, and salt until thoroughly combined. Set aside.

3   In a clean and dry bowl of a stand mixer fitted with the whisk attachment, whip the eggs and granulated sugar on medium-high speed until the mixture reaches the ribbon stage, 8 to 10 minutes. This results in a thick and pale yellow mixture. Whisk in the lychee extract.

*Continued*

4   Using a large sieve, sift one-third of the dry ingredients into the bowl with the egg mixture. Gently fold them into the egg mixture using a rubber spatula. Repeat the process twice more until all of the flour mixture is incorporated into the batter.

5   Measure ½ cup of the batter and add it to the medium bowl with the cooled butter. Proceed to whisk it into the butter until it becomes a homogenous mixture. Fold the tempered butter mixture into the remaining batter until well combined. Cover the bowl with plastic wrap and refrigerate overnight. Chilling the batter overnight is key for creating those classic madeleine humps.

6   Position a rack in the middle of the oven and preheat the oven to 350°F.

7   Place the remaining 2 tablespoons butter in a small microwave-safe bowl and microwave in 10-second intervals until completely melted. Using a pastry brush, brush the wells of a madeleine pan with the melted butter. Drop 1 heaping tablespoon of batter into each well. Bake for 10 to 12 minutes, or until the edges are golden brown. Immediately remove the madeleines from the pan and place shell-side up on a wire rack to cool completely. Repeat the process until all the madeleine batter is baked.

8   In a small saucepan, heat the lychee juice over medium-high heat. Once it reaches a boil, add the hibiscus tea bag and turn off the heat. Let the tea bag sit for at least 10 minutes. Discard the tea bag and pour the steeped juice in a small bowl.

9   In another small bowl, whisk together the powdered sugar and 3 tablespoons of the lychee juice, adding up to 1 more tablespoon of the lychee juice until it becomes a smooth glaze.

10   Take each madeleine and dip at a diagonal into the glaze. Put madeleines back on the wire rack and immediately sprinkle each with dried rose petals. Leave on the rack for at least 30 minutes, until the glaze has set. Serve at room temperature. Store any leftovers in an airtight container at room temperature for up to 3 days.

# Marshmallow-Filled Mamon

*Makes 20 cupcakes*

Goldilocks bakery cakes have made a lasting impression on me ever since I was a kid. The chain's mamon are no exception. I've always considered them to be S-tier snacks. The buttery soft mini sponge cakes are so good plain, but I do like the special variety with sugar and cheese on top more. As a family, we mostly went to Goldilocks to buy desserts for a special occasion. Whenever we'd go to run-of-the-mill grocery stores on a regular day, ten-year-old me (who craved cake constantly!) would look in the Hostess section for something to fill the Goldilocks void in my stomach. Twinkies, the oblong vanilla sponge cakes with creamy white filling, used to be my lunch box staple. Despite how much the filling made my teeth hurt from the sheer amount of sugar in it, it was my favorite part.

For my mamon recipe, I fused the concepts of Twinkies and mamon together with a bit of Marshmallow Fluff. Filling the centers of homemade sponge cakes with a store-bought meringue-like spread that tastes like the inside of a Twinkie helps to save time with mamon assembly. Shredded cheese on top of each mamon curbs the added sweetness of the filling, and is a nod to the special mamon variety.

## Cake

* I cup plus 2 tablespoons cake flour
* 1½ teaspoons baking powder
* ¼ teaspoon kosher salt
* 4 large eggs, at room temperature
* ⅓ cup whole milk, at room temperature
* ¾ teaspoon vanilla extract
* ¼ cup vegetable oil
* ¾ cup sugar
* ½ teaspoon cream of tartar

## Filling & Topping

* 1¼ cups Marshmallow Fluff
* 4 tablespoons (½ stick) unsalted butter, melted
* ¼ cup sugar
* I cup finely shredded Cheddar

## Cake

1   Position a rack in the middle of the oven and preheat the oven to 325°F. Line 20 cavities among two standard cupcake pans with paper liners and set aside.

2   In a small bowl, mix together the cake flour, baking powder, and salt until the baking powder is evenly distributed. Set aside.

*Continued*

3    Separate the eggs, placing the yolks in a large bowl and the egg whites in a clean and dry medium bowl.

4    Add the milk, vanilla, vegetable oil, and $1/4$ cup of the sugar to the egg yolks and whisk by hand. Slowly add in the flour mixture and continue to whisk until well combined.

5    Add the cream of tartar to the egg whites and beat with an electric hand mixer on medium-high speed until soft peaks form, 1 to 2 minutes. Gradually add in the remaining $1/2$ cup sugar and continue beating until stiff peaks form, another 1 to 2 minutes.

6    Using a rubber spatula, gently fold the meringue into the flour mixture in three batches, making sure each batch is fully incorporated into the batter before adding the next.

7    Divide the batter evenly among the prepared muffin pans, using about $1/4$ cup of batter per cavity.

8    Bake for 15 to 20 minutes, or until a toothpick inserted into the center of one cupcake comes out clean. Remove the cupcakes from the pans and transfer them to a wire rack to cool completely.

## Filling & Topping

9    Using an apple corer or a knife, hollow out a section that is about $3/4$ inch in diameter and $3/4$ of the depth of each cupcake. Fill each center with about 1 tablespoon of the Marshmallow Fluff.

10    Using a pastry brush, brush the tops of the cupcakes with the melted butter. Sprinkle each cupcake with sugar and a generous amount of shredded cheese. Store any leftovers in an airtight container in the fridge for up to 3 days.

# CANDIES

You don't have to be Willy Wonka to be able to make these candies at home. With a saucepan and a candy thermometer, you can whip up sweet treats in the comfort of your own kitchen.

# Yema Buckeyes

### *Makes 20 balls*

When the Spanish colonized the Philippines, many churches were constructed using egg whites as mortar. Hence, a slew of yolk-heavy recipes were invented to use up the excess yolks. These sweet, rich recipes have remained staples in Filipino households. For Christmas, my mom loves making yema, egg custard confections that are often rolled into tiny spheres and covered in a caramel that hardens so there's a slight crunch when you bite into them.

I've always been fascinated by and curious about the food culture in the Midwest. Ate Sydney attended Ohio State University for veterinary school, which made me think of buckeye candies. They're sweet peanut butter balls that are dipped in a coating of chocolate, and their circular shape reminds me of my mom's yema. Combining an American and Filipino classic in one appealed to me. Using dark chocolate balances the sweetness of the custard.

* 1 (14-ounce) can sweetened condensed milk
* 4 large egg yolks, at room temperature
* 1 tablespoon unsalted butter, at room temperature
* ½ teaspoon kosher salt
* 6 ounces dark chocolate (60% to 72% cacao), coarsely chopped
* 1 tablespoon coconut oil

1  Line a baking sheet with parchment paper. Set aside.

2  Combine the condensed milk, egg yolks, butter, and salt in a medium saucepan. Cook over low heat, stirring constantly with a rubber spatula, until the mixture turns into a thick dough, 12 to 15 minutes. Turn off the heat. Transfer the mixture to a medium bowl and let sit at room temperature for 30 minutes.

3  Roll the dough into 2-teaspoon-size balls and place them on the lined baking sheet. Chill the yema balls in the fridge for at least 1 hour.

4  Combine the chopped chocolate and coconut oil in a small microwave-safe bowl. Microwave for 30-second intervals, mixing between each round until the chocolate has melted completely.

5  Insert a toothpick into a yema ball and dip the yema ball in the chocolate. Make sure to leave a portion of the top uncoated to get that classic buckeye look. Shake off excess chocolate before placing the yema back on the baking sheet. Smooth over the toothpick hole with the back of a spoon. Repeat with the rest of the balls.

6  Return the baking sheet to the fridge. Let the buckeyes chill for at least 30 minutes to allow the chocolate to harden before serving. Store any leftovers in an airtight container in the fridge for up to 1 week.

# Matcha Pastillas

*Makes 32 pastillas*

No-bake recipes are the best for all of us who don't want to turn on the oven, especially when you live in an apartment without central A/C. These matcha pastillas are soft milk candies that pack a lot of flavor, and you don't need a stove or oven to make them. While traditional pastillas from Bulacan are made by cooking down carabao milk with sugar until the mixture forms a thick, chewy dough you can roll into cylinders, this recipe does away with the heat altogether. You'll still have rich, toothsome candies, but in a quarter of the time. Kneading the pastillas dough and shaping it into logs is quite therapeutic. By the end of making this recipe, you'll be excited to have these lying around to give to loved ones or enjoy yourself.

* 2¼ cups whole milk powder
* 2 tablespoons matcha powder
* ½ teaspoon kosher salt
* 1 (14-ounce) can sweetened condensed milk
* ¼ cup sugar, for rolling

1  Using a large sieve, sift the whole milk powder, matcha powder, and salt into a medium bowl. Mix the condensed milk into the sifted dry ingredients with a rubber spatula. Knead the pastillas dough by hand until the dry ingredients are fully incorporated, 1 to 2 minutes.

2  Line a baking sheet with parchment paper. Pour the sugar into a small bowl.

3  Scoop the dough into 1-tablespoon balls onto the lined baking sheet. Pick up one dough ball at a time, and roll each ball between your palms until it forms a log that is about 2½ inches long and ½ inch wide. Roll the finished log in the granulated sugar and return to the sheet.

4  Repeat until all the logs are formed. You can eat these as is now, or you can wrap each in 6 × 6-inch squares of cellophane. If wrapping in cellophane, place each log at the center edge of the square and roll up. Twist the ends to seal. Store at room temperature in an airtight container for up to 1 week.

# Spicy Bagoong Caramels

### *Makes 96 caramels*

Bagoong, in all its fermented shrimpy glory, is such a piquant addition to any dish or snack. I could eat it all day with sour slices of green mango or mixed into a tomato salad. Adding a touch of spicy sautéed bagoong makes this caramel a quartet of sweet, salty, savory, and spicy that you won't be able to forget. When looking for a jar of bagoong at your local Filipino grocery store for this recipe, go for the sautéed shrimp variety labeled as ginisang bagoong alamang or salted shrimp fry. Don't be confused with another type of dark brown bagoong called bagoong isda, which is made from fermented fish.

* Nonstick spray
* ½ cup heavy cream
* 2 tablespoons unsalted butter
* ¾ cup packed dark brown sugar
* 2 tablespoons light corn syrup
* I tablespoon spicy sautéed bagoong

1   Using nonstick spray, grease a silicone mold that has at least 96 square cavities. Each square should hold 2 milliliters' worth of caramel.

2   Place the cream, butter, brown sugar, corn syrup, 2 tablespoons water, and the bagoong in a medium saucepan. Cook over low heat, stirring frequently with a rubber spatula, until the mixture reaches a boil, 3 to 4 minutes.

3   Clip a candy thermometer to the saucepan. Continue stirring until the mixture reaches 240°F to 245°F. This can take 8 to 10 minutes.

4   Remove the pan from the heat and remove the candy thermometer.

5   Pour the caramel into the prepared molds, using the rubber spatula to evenly spread the mixture. Let the caramel squares cool to room temperature.

6   Cover the mold with a sheet of parchment paper and chill in the fridge overnight before wrapping each caramel in a square of wax or parchment paper. Store the caramels in an airtight container in the fridge for up to I month.

# Five-Spice Turrones de Casoy

*Makes 12 pieces*

When I was still living in San Jose, my favorite pretend game was re-creating the Eucharist. Before receiving my first Communion in second grade, I was always jealous of the adults who got to eat the wafer and drink the wine. My sister Ginelle and I would tear up pieces of the edible wafers that turrones de casoy came in, and we would give them to each other like the priests at mass. Turrones de casoy are candies inspired by the Spanish turrón, a nougat made with honey, egg whites, and nuts. They are typically made with cashews and wrapped in starch papers so that they don't stick to one another. I always loved that you could eat the papers of this treat that is from my parents' home province of Pampanga. Any time one of my relatives went back to the Philippines for a visit, they'd come back bearing gifts of turrones de casoy, dried watermelon seeds, and other snacks. If I ever saw the white tins with blue font from Ocampo Lansang Delicacies based in Santa Rita, Pampanga, I just knew I would be the first to finish the turrones de casoy in them.

For my version of turrones de casoy, I was inspired by a Chinese five-spice peanut brittle that I had made for Lao Gan Ma chili crisp cupcakes in September 2020. This brittle, infused with a mix of Sichuan peppercorns, fennel, cinnamon, anise seeds, and cloves, added a licorice-like dimension to my spicy dessert. Ever since I made that brittle, I knew that I wanted to incorporate five-spice into another candy. The sweet and floral honey in turrones de casoy tastes heavenly with this blend of spices. I buy wafer paper—made from potato starch, water, and vegetable oil—online for wrapping the nougat. If you search for the same paper that they use at bakeries to print out edible designs onto cakes, you can find it easily.

* Edible wafer paper sheets (see Headnote)
* I cup raw cashews
* ¼ cup cornstarch
* ¼ cup powdered sugar
* 2 large egg whites, at room temperature
* ½ cup honey
* I cup granulated sugar
* ¾ teaspoon five-spice powder
* ½ teaspoon kosher salt

1   Using kitchen scissors, cut twelve 3 × 8-inch rectangles from the wafer paper sheets and set aside.

2   Place the raw cashews in a large saucepan. Toast over medium-high heat, stirring frequently with a wooden spoon until lightly browned and fragrant, 4 to 6 minutes. Turn off the heat.

*Continued*

3   Transfer the toasted cashews to a cutting board and finely chop. Set aside.

4   Whisk together the cornstarch and powdered sugar in a small bowl. Sprinkle some of the mixture on a silicone mat and set aside.

5   Place the egg whites in a clean and dry medium bowl. Beat with an electric hand mixer on medium-high speed until they reach soft peaks, 1 to 2 minutes. Keep the bowl close to the stovetop.

6   Clip a candy thermometer to a medium saucepan. Place the honey, granulated sugar, five-spice powder, and salt in the saucepan over low heat and stir constantly until the sugar is dissolved and reaches the soft-crack stage, between 270°F and 290°F. If you take a spoonful of the syrup and drop it into a small bowl of cold water, you should be able to pull it between your fingers and see it form firm but pliable threads. This can take 5 to 7 minutes.

7   Ladle ¼ cup of the hot syrup into the medium bowl of whipped egg whites and whisk quickly to temper the whites.

8   Immediately stir the tempered egg whites into the saucepan using a rubber spatula. Continuously stir the mixture until the mixture reaches the 5-second ribbon stage, 14 to 16 minutes. When you lift your spatula and drizzle some of the mixture on the surface, monitor how long it takes for the ribbons to disappear. They will disappear in the first second initially, but cooking it longer will result in ribbons that disappear after waiting for 5 seconds.

9   Turn off the heat and fold in the chopped cashews. It's ideal if the cashews aren't cold upon folding because it will harden the mixture much faster. Immediately transfer the nougat mixture to the prepared silicone mat.

10   Sprinkle more of the cornstarch mixture on top, and using a rubber spatula, flatten into a 5 × 5-inch square that's ½ inch thick. While it's still warm and pliable, cut the square in half and cut across both halves into six equal rows. You should end up with twelve nougat rectangles total.

11   Wrap each nougat in a wafer paper rectangle by placing it in the center of the rectangle, rolling up, and then sealing the ends with a finger lightly dampened with some water. Be careful not to use too much water or the wafer paper will start to disintegrate. You need just enough to pinch the ends closed. Store them in an airtight container at room temperature for up to 2 weeks.

# Double-Toasted Coconut Marshmallows

*Makes 54 (2-inch square) marshmallows*

I just want to preface this recipe by saying that there's nothing wrong with store-bought marshmallows. I love having a bag on hand for s'mores, but it's nice having the flexibility of choosing what flavors you want when making them from scratch. The possibilities are endless! For my recipe, the mixture is flavored with coconut extract and then covered with coconut in two forms: toasted, unsweetened shredded coconut and latik (toasted coconut curds). The coconut coating adds a nutty crunch to otherwise pillowy-soft marshmallows. I like to use these marshmallows for the topping of my Tsokolate Pandesal Pudding (page 224). They turn nice and gooey when placing the chocolate bread pudding under the broiler. Instead of using a 12 × 18-inch baking sheet, you can also use a 9 × 9-inch square pan for thicker marshmallows. The final number of marshmallows depends on how big you want each marshmallow to be.

* Nonstick spray
* 3 (0.25-ounce) envelopes unflavored gelatin powder
* ²/₃ cup light corn syrup
* 2 cups sugar
* ¹/₂ teaspoon kosher salt
* I teaspoon coconut extract
* I³/₄ cups unsweetened shredded coconut
* ¹/₄ cup Latik (Toasted Coconut Curds, page 30)

1   Line a 12 × 18-inch baking sheet with plastic wrap and coat the plastic wrap with nonstick spray. Set aside.

2   Pour ¹/₂ cup of water into the bowl of a stand mixer fitted with the whisk attachment. Gently stir in the gelatin and let it bloom while you work on the sugar syrup.

3   Clip a candy thermometer to a medium saucepan. Combine ¹/₄ cup of water, the corn syrup, sugar, and salt in the saucepan.

4   Cook over medium-low heat, stirring the mixture occasionally with a rubber spatula, until the syrup reaches the soft-ball stage, between 235°F to 240°F. If you take a spoonful of the syrup

*Continued*

and drop it into a small bowl of cold water, the syrup should be able to form a soft ball. When you take it out of the water, the ball should lose its shape. This can take 15 to 18 minutes.

5    Once the syrup reaches the soft-ball stage, turn the stand mixer to low speed and gradually pour the hot syrup down the sides of the bowl. Be careful not to pour directly into the whisk to avoid splattering hot sugar. After all the syrup has been added, pour in the coconut extract.

6    Increase the speed to medium-high and whip until the marshmallow mixture thickens and turns white, 12 to 14 minutes.

7    Using a rubber spatula, spread the whipped mixture in an even layer on the lined baking sheet, making sure it reaches the edges of the sheet.

8    Spray the surface of the marshmallow slab with more nonstick spray. Cover with a sheet

*Continued*

of parchment paper. Let it cool and firm up at room temperature for at least 4 hours, preferably overnight.

9   When you're ready to cut up the marshmallows, toast the unsweetened shredded coconut in a large saucepan: Cook over medium-low heat, stirring frequently with a wooden spoon, until the flakes turn golden brown and fragrant, 10 to 12 minutes. Turn off the heat and transfer the coconut to a medium bowl.

10   Add the latik to the bowl and whisk until evenly incorporated into the unsweetened shredded coconut.

11   Spray the wheel of a pizza slicer with nonstick spray. Using the pizza slicer, cut the marshmallow slab into 2-inch squares. Roll the squares in the coconut mixture. Store the marshmallows in an airtight container at room temperature for up to 3 days.

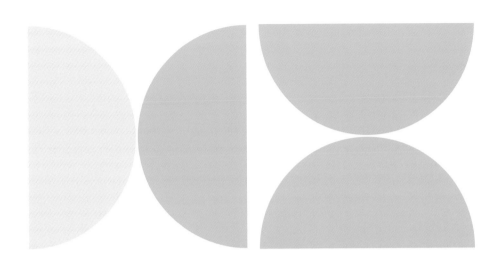

# PART III
## Stockton, California

*Swagapinos & the Scene*

In 2001, my family moved into a house in Stockton with just the five of us. My dad carpooled to work at NUMMI, which was a big Toyota manufacturing plant in Fremont. While he was working the graveyard shift, my mom was able to work nine to five at the University of the Pacific's accounting department. By choosing to live in the Central Valley, my parents were able to afford a mortgage for a home that they couldn't even fathom in the expensive Bay Area housing market. In some ways, it was kind of isolating not being in San Jose with my extended family anymore. However, we were still among a multitude of Filipinos. My parents had Filipino friends, and they had us hang out with their kids. My grandparents on my dad's side, Lolo Hugo and Lola Undi, even came to live with us in 2004.

At my elementary school, a majority of us students came from low-income backgrounds, so we qualified for free or reduced-price lunch. I looked forward to munching on my Smucker's Uncrustables PB&J in between bites of the Eng Bee Tin *ube hopia* I brought from home. There was a large Latinx community and scores of first-generation Filipino Americans who were also in my classes. Even the popular kids were members of a *swagapino* sibling dynasty. I remember having the biggest crush on one of them who was my age. He had spiky hair, those Italian charm bracelets that linked together in silver squares, and the coolest Air Jordans. When I was in first grade, we chased each other around the playground during recess. He called me *pangit* and then I burst into tears. Needless to say, I got over him eventually.

Years later, I realized that the community I was surrounded by was no coincidence. There's a Little Manila in downtown Stockton, which has a long history of Manongs who immigrated from the early 1900s to the 1930s to work in the fields. They fought for better labor conditions for agricultural workers. Generations of Filipinos have lived in Stockton, and I feel grateful now to have experienced growing up there for most of my youth and adolescence.

As I reached middle school, the nerd in me was hell-bent on being an overachiever. Much like Frankie Muniz in *Malcolm in the Middle*, I thought that I was the smart one in my dysfunctional family. I also had a bad case of middle child syndrome because it felt like my parents just didn't take any notice of me. My mom would often fail to call me by the right name, mixing it up with my siblings' even though their names weren't even remotely close to mine. Teachers at school were constantly comparing my sister Ginelle and me since she was only three years my senior. In a fit of competitive rage, I felt like I needed to be the best. I had straight A's all the way into high school, and I even got "Most Likely to Succeed" as my superlative.

No matter how much Fall Out Boy I listened to at sixteen years old or how deep I could get my side-part bangs, I felt like I couldn't set myself apart enough from everyone else at school either. When my family and I went to Weberstown Mall, I made a beeline toward Hot Topic any chance that I got. It was like I had the opposite problem of hyper-assimilation. I wanted to be seen as a unique individual. I knew that I wasn't like my parents, who were born and raised in the Philippines, but I was also not really like the other Filipino teens around me. They were break-dancing, blasting hip-hop, and playing their ukuleles in the quad between classes. The guys banded together to take turns doing donuts in the parking lot. Even though I had Filipino friends, it felt like this echelon of Filipinos was a clique that I was too nerdy and weird to join. At the most basic level, I was a Filipino scene girl walking among swagapinos.

Going to high school with mostly other students of color did, however, make me feel more comfortable with my identity. I'm relieved that I didn't have the inverse experience of being the only Filipino kid in a predominantly white town. There was no teasing from other kids about a stinky lunch box or a desire to be white instead. With that comfort, I was also complacent in thinking that just a few factors defined Filipino-ness: big families, Catholicism, and freakishly good singing abilities. Instead of putting down my culture because of apparent self-loathing, I kind of took it for granted. Looking back, I wish I'd engaged more critically with my Filipino heritage than passively accepting it at surface-level as part of my daily existence. Now I know that being Filipino isn't just an aggregation of silly stereotypes. Being Filipino means that I must actively choose resistance and continue to uplift my community. I am special because I am Filipino.

Even though my teen years were an emotional roller coaster, I found a love for baking at thirteen that helped ground me. When I first got into baking as a hobby, I'd make do with using just a whisk and brute force to try cake recipes. When I was seventeen, my parents got me a KitchenAid stand mixer for Christmas. Being a stand mixer owner became my whole personality. When I wasn't running Dumbledore's Army (our school's first and only *Harry Potter* fan club) or volunteering at Key Club events, I was in the kitchen making desserts. I started baking mini cheesecakes to add to the dessert table at family parties. The success of these paved the way for me to get inventive with flavor combinations like the ube and sesame cracker cheesecake bars (page 133). For the raffle at a tsunami relief benefit concert in 2011, I baked a set of peanut butter cupcakes other students could win as a prize. Instead of just being a dork, I was a dork who could bake.

# PASTRIES & PIES

There's an idiom that anything typical in America can be "as American as apple pie." With the US occupation of the Philippines, this penchant for apple pie was popularized and later adapted with native fruit fillings. Thus, pies containing tropical ingredients like pineapple and buko (young coconut) have become beloved desserts in our culture.

# Pumpkin Hopia

### *Makes 24 hopia*

Every time I wander along the aisles of Seafood City, I end up spending the most time in the refrigerated section looking for my beloved Eng Bee Tin hopia. Hopia are Filipino flaky pastries that are similar to Chinese mooncakes. They're usually filled with sweetened yellow mung beans or even ube halaya. However, for this recipe, I opted for a pumpkin variation replete with spices that harken back to the classic Thanksgiving pumpkin pie. Instead of just having one pie to look forward to in November, these pumpkin hopia can be easily served anytime as snacks throughout the year.

## Pumpkin Filling

* 1 (15-ounce) can 100% pure pumpkin
* 1/2 cup packed dark brown sugar
* 1/2 teaspoon kosher salt
* 1 1/2 teaspoons ground cinnamon
* 1/2 teaspoon ground nutmeg
* 1/2 teaspoon ground ginger
* 1/8 teaspoon ground cloves
* 2 tablespoons cornstarch
* 2 large eggs, at room temperature
* 1 teaspoon vanilla extract

## Dough 1

* 1 cup all-purpose flour, plus more for dusting
* 1/2 teaspoon kosher salt
* 8 tablespoons (1 stick) unsalted butter, cold, cut into tablespoon-size pieces
* 1/4 cup plus 2 tablespoons ice water

## Dough 2

* 1/2 cup all-purpose flour
* 1 tablespoon granulated sugar

* 1/4 teaspoon kosher salt
* 4 tablespoons (1/2 stick) unsalted butter, cold, cut into tablespoon-size pieces

## Egg Wash

* 2 large egg yolks, at room temperature
* 1 tablespoon whole milk, at room temperature

## Pumpkin Filling

1   In a medium saucepan, stir together the pumpkin, brown sugar, salt, cinnamon, nutmeg, ginger, cloves, and cornstarch with a wooden spoon.

2   In a small bowl, whisk the eggs until lightly beaten. Set aside, but keep the bowl close to your stovetop.

3   Cook the pumpkin mixture over medium-high heat, stirring frequently with a wooden spoon until it reaches a boil, 5 to 7 minutes.

4   Spoon 1/4 cup of the hot pumpkin mixture into the small bowl and quickly whisk to temper the

eggs. Whisk another ¼ cup of the pumpkin mixture into the bowl, and immediately pour the mixture back into the saucepan. Reduce the heat to low and continue to cook, stirring constantly, until the mixture reaches a boil, 3 to 4 minutes. Once the mixture starts to get very thick and clump together, turn off the heat. Stir in the vanilla.

5   Scrape the filling into a medium bowl and let it cool at room temperature for 15 minutes. Cover with plastic wrap and store in the fridge for at least 1 hour before assembling the hopia.

## Dough 1

6   Pulse the flour, salt, and butter together in a food processor, until the mixture turns into pea-size crumbs, 10 to 15 pulses. Sprinkle in the water and pulse until the mixture forms a dough ball, 11 to 14 pulses.

7   Take dough out and flatten into a 1-inch-thick disc. Wrap in plastic wrap and place it in the fridge to rest for at least 30 minutes.

## Dough 2

8   Place the flour, sugar, salt, and butter in the food processor and blitz until the mixture forms pea-size crumbs, 25 to 30 pulses. Set aside until you're ready to assemble the hopia.

## Egg Wash

9   In a small bowl, whisk together the egg yolks and milk until it becomes a homogenous mixture. Set aside.

## Assembly

10   Position a rack in the middle of the oven and preheat the oven to 350°F. Line a baking sheet with a silicone mat.

11   Lightly flour a rolling pin and your work surface. Take Dough 1 out of the fridge and plop it on your work surface. Roll out the dough into a 10 × 12-inch rectangle, about ⅛ inch thick. Make sure to pick up the dough and occasionally sprinkle some flour between rolls so that it doesn't stick.

12   Sprinkle Dough 2 evenly over the surface of the Dough 1 rectangle. Lightly press Dough 2 with your fingertips so it adheres to Dough 1.

13   Starting from one short end, fold one-third of the dough over the center. Take the opposite end and fold over the two layers. This is a single letter fold. Roll the dough back out into a 10 × 12-inch rectangle again. Repeat this letter fold process twice more.

14   Using a pizza slicer, divide the rectangle of dough lengthwise in half. Starting from the long end, tightly roll each piece into a log.

15   Cut each log into 12 equal slices to create 24 total pieces of dough.

16   Place one dough ball on your work surface. Cover the other dough balls with plastic wrap so that they don't dry out. With your rolling pin, roll the ball as thin as possible. It should be a circle that's at least 4 inches in diameter.

17   Take the pumpkin filling out of the fridge. Place 1 tablespoon of filling in the center of the

*Continued*

dough circle. Pick up the edges of the dough circle and pleat them so that they enclose the filling. Pinch the dough at the top to seal.

18 Place the hopia, pleated side down, into a 2-inch round cookie cutter to lightly flatten and shape it into a disc. It should look like a little hockey puck. Place it on the prepared baking sheet.

19 Repeat the process with the remaining dough balls and filling, placing the hopia 1 inch apart from one another.

20 Using a pastry brush, brush the tops and sides of each hopia with the egg wash before popping them into the oven.

21 Bake for 10 minutes and then take the baking sheet out of the oven to do a second egg wash coat. After brushing the tops and sides of each hopia with the egg wash, place them back in the oven to bake for another 10 to 12 minutes, or until golden brown. Transfer the baking sheet to a wire rack to cool completely. Store in an airtight container in the fridge for up to 4 days.

# Giant Cashew Tart

*Makes 10 servings*

Whenever I bring back pasalubong, or gifts to give to family and friends, from the Philippines, I make sure to save a few cellophane-wrapped cashew tarts for myself. The bite-size buttery shells hold a cashew and caramel mixture that is out of this world. I only wish that I could also buy a giant version of the tarts to make them last longer. By baking one tart in an 11-inch pan, I've solved my main problem of not having enough to go around.

## Crust

* 1½ cups all-purpose flour, plus more for dusting
* 1¼ cups powdered sugar
* ¼ teaspoon kosher salt
* 8 tablespoons (1 stick) unsalted butter, cold, cut into tablespoon-size pieces
* 1 large egg yolk, cold
* 2 tablespoons ice water

## Filling

* 1½ cups raw cashews
* 1½ cups granulated sugar
* 1½ cups heavy cream, at room temperature
* 3 tablespoons unsalted butter, at room temperature
* 3 large eggs, at room temperature
* 1 teaspoon vanilla extract

## Crust

1   Add the flour, powdered sugar, salt, and butter to a food processor. Pulse until the mixture forms pea-size crumbs, 10 to 12 pulses. Add in the egg yolk and ice water. Process until the mixture forms a dough ball, 20 to 25 pulses.

2   Take dough out and flatten into a 1-inch-thick disc. Wrap in plastic wrap and place it in the fridge to rest for at least 30 minutes.

3   Lightly flour a rolling pin and your work surface. Take the dough out of the fridge and plop it on your work surface. Roll out the dough into a 13-inch circle, about ⅛ inch thick. Make sure to pick up the dough and occasionally sprinkle some flour between rolls so that it doesn't stick.

4   Carefully lay the dough circle over an 11-inch tart shell with a removable bottom. Press the dough evenly into the bottom and up the sides of the pan. Cut away any excess overhang. If you have some holes, you can use these extra pieces to patch up your dough.

*Continued*

5   Prick the surface of the dough all over with a fork. This is called docking, and will prevent your tart dough from puffing up while baking. Transfer the tart shell to the fridge to chill for at least 30 minutes.

6   Position an oven rack in the middle of the oven and preheat the oven to 400°F.

7   Line the chilled tart shell with aluminum foil and fill it with pie weights. If you don't have pie weights, you can use rice or dried beans instead. Place the tart pan on a baking sheet and bake for 10 minutes.

8   Take the pan out of the oven to remove the foil and pie weights. Return the tart shell to the oven to bake for another 7 to 10 minutes, until it is lightly golden brown. Transfer to a wire rack to cool. Reduce the oven temperature to 325°F while you make your filling.

## Filling

9   Place the raw cashews in a large saucepan set over medium-high heat. Stir frequently with a wooden spoon for 4 to 6 minutes, or until lightly browned and fragrant. Turn off the heat.

10   Transfer the toasted cashews to a cutting board and finely chop. Set aside.

11   Place the sugar in the saucepan. Cook over low heat, stirring frequently with a rubber spatula, until it completely melts and turns golden brown, 14 to 16 minutes.

12   Immediately stir in the heavy cream and butter. Be careful as the caramel is likely to bubble up. If caramel hardens upon contact with the other ingredients, continue cooking for 6 to 8 more minutes, or until it melts completely again.

13   Transfer the mixture to a large bowl and let cool to room temperature.

14   Once completely cooled and no longer warm to touch, whisk in about two-thirds of the chopped cashews, the eggs, and vanilla until well combined.

15   Pour the caramel-cashew mixture into the partially baked tart shell. Sprinkle the top with the remaining chopped cashews.

16   Bake for 27 to 30 minutes, or until the center looks just set and the edges of the crust are golden brown. Transfer to a rack to cool completely before slicing. Store any leftovers in an airtight container in the fridge for up to 4 days.

# So You Want to Be a Blog Star

Growing up, I gravitated toward Food Network programming as a comfort watch when I'd run out of *Lizzie McGuire* episodes. I had reruns of *Unwrapped* queued up on our DVR. I was always fascinated by how nostalgic treats like Hostess Cupcakes and Peeps Marshmallows were produced in factories. My favorite show, hands down, was *Ace of Cakes*. I drew up diagrams of what my ideal *matryoshka* doll birthday cake would be if I ever got one made by the team at Charm City Cakes. Mind you, Baltimore was so far away, and I don't even think I could afford one of their cakes now. I spent hours penning new show concepts I could pitch and thinking that would be my ticket to working at the network one day.

When I wasn't captivated by the glitz and glamour of food television, I was surfing the web and perusing my favorite food blogs. *Smitten Kitchen*, *Brown Eyed Baker*, and *Annie's Eats* were all my go-tos. Our family laptop was bogged down with bookmarked recipes that I had every intention of making. Across the board, I was idolizing white women in their early thirties whose lives seemed perfect. I thrived on reading stories about their darling kitchen remodels and kids' dinosaur-themed birthday parties at the start of each post. In hindsight, it was very Jennifer Garner in *13 Going on 30* of me to think that was what the future had in store. Not to mention, I didn't look remotely like any of those bloggers.

I found another online community in 2009, Allrecipes, that solidified my love for baking. Anyone could sign up to write recipes, read other users' recipes, and leave reviews. As a kid in middle school who spent too much time on Yahoo! Answers, I was already sold on the premise of lightly engaging with random people on the internet. I was such an active user back then, but by no means was I the face behind a famous account. It was a serotonin boost anytime I got upvotes on my chocolate chip cookie and brownie recipe reviews. I recently stumbled upon my old profile, which I thought was long gone. This is the semi-cringe bio from my profile that's still up today:

"I'm Abi and I love *Harry Potter*. It's been an obsession of mine for the last 6 years:) I'm a person that puts in her all no matter what she is doing."

Although I can't personally log in to my Allrecipes account anymore (my email was deactivated after I forgot the password to it), I still have a massive appreciation for this site and all the food bloggers who share their recipes. I was just so young when I really got into baking that I didn't have an allowance or disposable income to buy my own cookbooks. Hence, the internet was where I taught myself basic baking skills. My mom could show me how to make yema, but she wasn't the one who liked Applebee's butter pecan blondies so much that she'd attempt to bake them herself from a blog post. That was all me. Even before I started my baking blog, the aspect of discovery by happenstance really drew me into this world. The possibility that someone could stumble upon your words and sweet creations at any given moment was, and still is, such a romantic way of thinking about food writing online. It's way more than just an SEO numbers game.

# Pacific Beach Pie

*Makes 8 servings*

Hailing from North Carolina, the Atlantic Beach pie is a lemon-lime custard pie with a saltine cracker crust. I came across a post about Atlantic Beach pie when I was scrolling through the archive of one of my favorite baking blogs, *Hummingbird High*. The way Michelle, the baker behind the blog, described the pie was music to my ears. I love citrus and any dessert that has a salty component. For my recipe, I choose to add calamansi juice and SkyFlakes Crackers instead. SkyFlakes are thick wheat crackers that are lightly salted, and I grew up eating them as a simple snack. These Filipino staples taste wonderful together, especially with homemade whipped cream. Since fresh calamansi isn't always easy to find in New York, I use a combination of oranges, lemons, and limes for zesting and candying. For the candied citrus topping, it helps to do this step the night before since you want to have time for the slices to dry. If you have fresh calamansi, you can utilize them instead. You would need to use approximately 16 fresh calamansi to get the 4 ounces of juice you need for the filling.

## Candied Citrus & Topping

* I whole lime
* I whole lemon
* 2 cups granulated sugar
* Zest of I orange, for decoration

## Crust

* 1½ cups SkyFlakes Cracker crumbs (from about 23 crackers)
* 6 tablespoons unsalted butter, melted
* ¼ cup granulated sugar

## Filling

* I (14-ounce) can sweetened condensed milk
* 4 large egg yolks, at room temperature
* 4 ounces frozen calamansi juice, thawed
* Zest of I lime
* Zest of I lemon
* ½ teaspoon kosher salt
* I teaspoon vanilla extract

## Whipped Cream Topping

* I cup heavy cream, cold
* ¼ cup powdered sugar, sifted
* I teaspoon vanilla extract

## Candied Citrus

1   Slice the lime and lemon as thin as possible with a knife or mandoline.

2   Set a wire rack over a baking sheet and set aside. Combine 2 cups water and the sugar in a large saucepan. Cook over medium-high heat,

*Continued*

stirring occasionally with a rubber spatula, until it reaches a boil, 4 to 5 minutes.

3   Once the mixture is at a boil, add in the lime and lemon slices. Reduce the heat to low and continue to cook until the rinds and piths are translucent, 55 to 60 minutes.

4   Transfer the candied slices to the wire rack to cool and dry overnight at room temperature.

## Crust

5   Position an oven rack in the middle of the oven and preheat the oven to 350°F.

6   In a medium bowl, whisk together the SkyFlakes Cracker crumbs, butter, and sugar. Press into a 9-inch pie pan (regular, not deep dish!). Use the bottom of a cup to evenly press the crumb mixture into the bottom and up the sides of the pan.

7   Bake the pie crust for 12 to 15 minutes, or until the edges are lightly browned. Transfer to a wire cooling rack. Leave the oven on.

## Filling

8   Whisk the condensed milk, egg yolks, calamansi juice, lime zest, lemon zest, salt, and vanilla in a medium bowl until well combined. Pour directly onto the slightly cooled pie crust.

9   Bake for 15 to 18 minutes, or until the center has a slight wobble but the edges are set. Transfer to a wire rack to cool at room temperature until it's cool enough to handle. Cover the top with plastic wrap and transfer to the fridge to chill for at least 4 hours, preferably overnight.

## Whipped Cream Topping

10   In a medium bowl, beat the heavy cream, powdered sugar, and vanilla with an electric hand mixer on medium-high speed until stiff peaks form, 3 to 4 minutes. Cover the bowl with plastic wrap and store in the fridge until you're ready to decorate the pie.

## Assembly

11   Take the pie out of the fridge.

12   Using a piping bag fitted with a 4B star tip, pipe a shell border of whipped cream around the edges of the pie. Pipe more whipped cream in the center of the pie.

13   Adorn the pie with the candied lemon and lime slices on top of the whipped cream.

14   Sprinkle orange zest all over the pie and serve cold. Store any leftovers in the fridge in an airtight container for up to 3 days.

# Mango Float Cream Puffs

### *Makes 26 cream puffs*

As a kid, I distinctly remember sneaking away from my parents' cart at Costco to prowl around the sample tables. I would go back multiple times just to have bites of the frozen cream puffs in those plastic tubs. When I got older, I never missed an opportunity to stop by Beard Papa's for more cream puffs. Beard Papa's is an international chain that specializes in cream puffs alone, and I'd often find them in the food court of a nearby mall. I am a cream puff fiend, and it's a game-changer being able to make them at home.

Mango float, or mango royale, is a Filipino icebox cake that has layers of whipped cream, graham crackers, and ripe Carabao mango. For individual portions, I opted to use cream puffs as edible mini bowls. The craquelin topping adds an extra crunch and an element of sweetness. It's a simple no-bake dessert where the mango is the star. If you can't find the Carabao variety, I recommend their descendant—Champagne, or Ataulfo, mangoes—as an alternative. Both varieties of mangoes are soft, have golden yellow skin when ripe, and are shaped like kidney beans. A big difference between the two is that Carabao mangoes are sweeter (they're actually the sweetest mangoes in the world according to *Guinness*!).

## Craquelin

* 8 tablespoons (I stick) unsalted butter, at room temperature
* 1/2 cup packed dark brown sugar
* I cup all-purpose flour
* 1/4 teaspoon kosher salt

## Choux Pastry

* 1/4 cup whole milk, at room temperature
* 8 tablespoons (I stick) unsalted butter, at room temperature
* I tablespoon granulated sugar
* 1/4 teaspoon kosher salt
* I cup all-purpose flour, plus more for dusting
* 4 large eggs, at room temperature

## Whipped Cream

* I cup heavy cream, cold
* 1/4 cup sweetened condensed milk, cold

## Assembly

* 6 1/2 graham cracker sheets, broken into squares
* 2 medium mangoes, peeled and cut into 1/4-inch dice

## Craquelin

1   Place the butter and brown sugar in the bowl of a stand mixer fitted with the paddle

*Continued*

attachment. Cream on medium-high speed until light and fluffy, 3 to 4 minutes.

2    Turn the mixer down to the lowest speed. Gradually add the flour and salt until all of the dry ingredients are incorporated, 2 to 3 minutes.

3    Dump the dough out of the stand mixer onto a sheet of plastic wrap. With your hands, press the clumps together and shape into a 6 × 8-inch rectangle. Wrap it all up in the plastic wrap.

4    Transfer the dough to the freezer and chill for at least 15 minutes.

5    Line a baking sheet with parchment paper. Lightly flour a rolling pin and your work surface. Take the craquelin dough out of the freezer and roll about $1/8$ inch thick. Cut out circles using a 2-inch round cookie cutter and transfer to the prepared baking sheet.

6    Gather and reroll the scraps to cut out more circles. Repeat the process until you have 26 circles. Store the circles in the freezer to keep them from melting while you make the choux pastry.

## Choux Pastry

7    Position a rack in the middle of the oven and preheat the oven to 375°F. Line a baking sheet with a silicone mat.

8    In a medium saucepan, combine the milk, $3/4$ cup water, the butter, sugar, and salt. Cook over medium-high heat, stirring occasionally with a wooden spoon, until the butter is completely melted and the mixture reaches a rolling boil, 2 to 3 minutes.

9    Turn off the heat and immediately stir in the flour. Stir vigorously until the mixture starts pulling away from the sides of the pot, 15 to 20 seconds.

10    Let the mixture cool for 5 minutes while still in the saucepan. Stir in the eggs, one at a time, until the mixture turns smooth and glossy. To check if it has the right piping consistency, take your wooden spoon, dip it in the dough, and pull it upright. The dough should form a V shape at the end of the spoon.

11    Transfer the dough to a piping bag fitted with a large round tip. Pipe mounds that are 2 inches wide and 1 inch tall, spacing them about 1 inch apart on the prepared baking sheet.

12    Take the craquelin circles out of the freezer. Gently place a craquelin circle directly on top of each choux mound.

13    Place the baking sheet in the oven and bake for 25 to 30 minutes, or until the shells have puffed up and are golden brown.

14    Remove the baking sheet from the oven and turn off the heat. Turn each shell over and pierce the bottom with a knife inserted about halfway into the puff. Be careful not to cut through to the craquelin top!

15    With the shells bottom-side up, place the baking sheet back in the oven with the door cracked slightly open for about 10 minutes. This step helps to release the steam inside each puff and dry them out.

*Continued*

16   After the l0 minutes are up, transfer the shells to a wire rack to cool completely.

## Whipped Cream

17   Pour the heavy cream into a large bowl. Using an electric hand mixer, whip the cream on medium-high speed until soft peaks form, about l minute.

18   Add the condensed milk. Whip until stiff peaks form and the condensed milk is fully mixed into the cream, about l to 2 minutes.

19   Place the bowl of sweetened cream in the fridge until you're ready to assemble the cream puffs.

## Assembly

20   Cut each puff in half. Line the puff bottoms alongside their coordinating tops.

21   Divide each graham cracker sheet into 8 equal squares. Place a graham cracker square on each puff bottom.

22   Take the bowl of whipped cream out of the fridge and transfer to a piping bag fitted with a IM star tip. Pipe about $1/2$ tablespoon of the cream on top of each graham cracker square. Place $1/2$ tablespoon of diced mango on top of the whipped cream layer. Pipe another $1/2$ tablespoon of cream on top of the diced mango.

23   Place another graham cracker square on top of the whipped cream. Place the tops of the shells back on the last graham cracker layer.

24   Serve immediately. Alternatively, you can chill the cream puffs in the fridge for 3 to 4 hours before serving. The graham cracker layers soften like a traditional mango float.

# Roasted Kamote Scones

*Makes 8 scones*

One of my parents' tricks is wrapping Japanese sweet potatoes with wet paper towels and turning them into mini desserts with a zap of the microwave. They cut each cooked kamote into rounds, and then carefully peel back the skin. You can still see the steam when you bite into a slice. Whenever I'd ask for one, I'd sprinkle sugar on top for extra sweetness. Inspired by my parents' love for these Japanese sweet potatoes and a yearning for scones I had in England when I studied abroad in the summer of 2016, I came up with a roasted kamote scone recipe that is the best of both worlds.

Even though these roasted kamote scones have a few more steps, I think my parents would still enjoy them. They don't normally go for scones or pastries that have cloying icings or glazes on them, so the flecks of crunchy pearl sugar would be a welcome change. While my parents' microwave cooking method is quicker, I like to roast the sweet potatoes because I think they have a deeper, more caramel-like flavor after baking in the oven. These scones are the perfect breakfast snack to go with coffee and tea.

* 2 medium Japanese sweet potatoes
* 1/3 cup buttermilk, cold
* 1/4 cup maple syrup
* 1 teaspoon vanilla extract
* 2 1/4 cups all-purpose flour
* 1/2 teaspoon kosher salt
* 1/4 cup packed dark brown sugar
* 2 teaspoons baking powder
* 1/4 teaspoon baking soda
* 8 tablespoons (1 stick) unsalted butter, cold, cut into tablespoon-size pieces
* 1/4 cup cold heavy cream, for brushing
* 2 tablespoons pearl sugar

1   Position a rack in the middle of the oven and preheat the oven to 400°F. Line one baking sheet with parchment paper.

2   Wash and scrub the Japanese sweet potatoes in the sink.

3   Dry with a paper towel and prick them all over with the tines of a fork. Place pricked potatoes on the parchment-lined baking sheet.

4   Bake for 45 to 50 minutes, or until each potato is cooked all the way through and tender. When you insert a fork into the middle of one, it should go in with no resistance. Turn off the oven and transfer the sheet to a wire cooling rack. Let the potatoes cool on the sheet for 10 minutes.

*Continued*

5    Peel each potato and place the flesh in a medium bowl. Mash with a fork until smooth and let cool to room temperature.

6    Once cooled, measure out ½ cup of the mashed sweet potato and place it in a large measuring cup. If there is any of the mash left over, it's a great snack to have while you're baking. Mix in the buttermilk, maple syrup, and vanilla. Set aside. With the rack still positioned in the middle of the oven, preheat the oven to 400°F. Line one baking sheet with a silicone mat.

7    Whisk the flour, salt, brown sugar, baking powder, and baking soda in a large bowl until well combined. Dump the contents of the bowl onto a work surface.

8    Using a pastry cutter, blend the butter into the flour mixture until it resembles pea-size crumbs.

9    Add the sweet potato mixture to the crumbs. Stir by hand and gently knead about 5 times. Flatten and shape the dough into an 8-inch round circle. Cut the dough into 8 equal wedges.

10   Place each scone on the prepared baking sheet. Using a pastry brush, coat the tops of the scones with the heavy cream. Sprinkle the tops with the pearl sugar.

11   Bake for 15 to 17 minutes, or until golden brown. Remove the scones from the baking sheet and transfer them to a wire rack to cool completely before serving. Store any leftovers in an airtight container at room temperature for up to 3 days.

# Thirty-Love

"Make sure you don't get too dark!" my mom would yell out whenever I'd leave the house smelling like sunscreen to go to tennis practice. Much to my mom's dismay, I started playing for the girls' tennis team during my junior year. Conditioning happened during the summer, and she was not happy about all the time I was spending outdoors. This seems like it wouldn't make any sense because shouldn't she be relieved that I was getting exercise and adding an extracurricular to my college applications? Nope. She just didn't like the fact that I'd get even more tan.

Ever since I was little, I'd go to Filipino grocery stores with my parents, and to get to the checkout, you'd pass by the aisles of skincare products. I'd be perplexed to see bottles of whitening soap and creams. Whenever we'd watch teleseryes on The Filipino Channel, both my mom and dad would point out the many fair-skinned actresses on the screen. These soap opera characters really had my parents mesmerized and tuning in to watch

every evening. My parents would tell me that if I were lighter, I could be a star in the Philippines. I knew that this wasn't unique to my parents, but a longstanding consequence of colonization. Stemming from a pressure to meet Western beauty standards, colorism is such a widespread issue in the Filipino community.

As damaging as this was to my self-esteem, I loved my brown skin. Being *morena*, naturally having brown skin, was a constant reminder of where I came from. I was born with sun-kissed skin, which I didn't need spray tans or extra-dark foundation to mimic. I never wanted to try any pseudo-remedies to make me whiter. When I think back on my tennis days, what good would it have done to quit a sport just because of a tan? No matter what insidious remarks my mom directed at me, I enjoyed playing tennis.

It is no exaggeration to say that I was a mediocre tennis player at best. I didn't grow up playing tennis at all, and I didn't have an athletic bone in my gangly body. My coach, Mr. Furtado, was really patient in correcting my form and helping me become a stronger player. Even though I had middling personal stats, our team had an undefeated winning streak. I remember leaving class early to go to one of our away matches, and as I was power walking to the van, someone who I didn't even know saw me in my tennis uniform and wished me luck. Our team became back-to-back Valley Oak League champions, and it made my whole 2011.

The tennis girls became some of my closest friends. We were exhausted and reeked of sweat after every game, but I looked forward to eating dinners that consisted of greasy slices of Mountain Mike's Pizza and double-doubles at In-N-Out together. During my first season, I baked a cookies & cream birthday cake for my teammate Sam's birthday. Haruna, a Japanese exchange student also on the team, and I ran into each other years later by chance at Shinagawa Station in Tokyo. She later showed my family and me around Nara, and I'm still so grateful for that moment of pure serendipity on a crowded train platform. Chelsea, who was our team captain our senior year, would sometimes give me a lift home after tennis practice. We'd drive for five minutes to get gas, and end up sitting parked in my driveway for what felt like hours just gossiping–peak suburban pastime! I love that when I'm visiting California to this day, she'll pick me up from my parents' house just so that we can hang out. Granted, I have my driver's license now, but relying solely on the subway for transportation in New York has made me terrified of getting behind the wheel.

If you see my old prom pictures, you'll see me grinning ear to ear with bold tan lines where my tennis uniform used to be. While those lines have mostly faded, I'll always be a proud morena.

# Buko Pie Lollipops

### *Makes 18 pie lollipops*

I've heard that the best buko—or young coconut—pie in the Philippines comes from Laguna, southeast of Manila, where it was invented. This double-crusted flaky pie contains a creamy filling that features young coconut meat, which is soft and jellylike, with a mild sweetness. I hope to visit Laguna one day, but I've only been able to try this delicacy at my local Goldilocks, my favorite Filipino bakery chain. This pie is so good that I will often go back for seconds to have another slice. I wanted to make buko pie in grab-and-go sizes, so I opted for serving them as lollipops. My favorite part is that you don't need to bother with a fork or pie cutter to have a bite (or two, or three!).

## Buko Filling

* ⅓ cup young coconut water
* 2 tablespoons cornstarch
* 1 (16-ounce) package frozen shredded buko, thawed and drained
* ½ cup sweetened condensed milk
* ¼ teaspoon kosher salt

## Pie Dough

* 2½ cups all-purpose flour, plus more for dusting
* 1¼ teaspoons kosher salt
* ½ pound (2 sticks) unsalted butter, cold, cut into tablespoon-size pieces
* ¼ cup plus 2 tablespoons ice water

## Egg Wash and Assembly

* 2 large egg yolks, at room temperature
* 1 tablespoon whole milk, at room temperature
* 18 lollipop sticks

## Buko Filling

1   In a small measuring cup, whisk the young coconut water and cornstarch until there are no lumps.

2   Combine the thawed buko, condensed milk, salt, and the coconut water mixture in a medium saucepan. Cook over medium-low heat, stirring frequently with a rubber spatula, until the filling thickens to a pudding consistency, 8 to 10 minutes.

3   Transfer to a medium bowl and directly cover the surface of the custard with plastic wrap to prevent a skin from forming. Let cool at room temperature for 15 minutes, and then chill in the fridge for at least 1 hour.

## Pie Dough

4   Pulse 1½ cups of the flour, the salt, and butter in a food processor until all the flour is coated in butter, 30 to 35 pulses.

*Continued*

5   Add the remaining 1 cup flour and process the mixture until it turns into pea-sized crumbs, 5 to 10 pulses.

6   Sprinkle in the water and process until it forms a dough ball, 5 to 10 pulses.

7   Take the dough out and flatten into a 1-inch-thick disc. Wrap in plastic wrap and place it in the fridge to rest for at least 1 hour.

## Egg Wash

8   In a small bowl, whisk together the egg yolks and milk until it becomes a homogenous mixture. Set aside.

## Assembly

9   Position a rack in the middle of the oven and preheat the oven to 350°F. Line two baking sheets with silicone mats.

10   Lightly flour a rolling pin and your work surface. Take the chilled pie dough out of the fridge and divide it in half. Return one half to the fridge and plop the other on your work surface. Roll the dough out about $1/8$ inch thick.

11   Using a $2^{1}/_{2}$-inch round cookie cutter, cut out circles of dough. Gather and reroll the scraps until you have 18 circles. Place 9 circles on each of the lined baking sheets, giving enough space between rows for the sticks.

12   Lightly flour your rolling pin and work surface again. Take the other half of the dough out of the fridge and plop it on your work surface. Roll the dough out about $1/8$ inch thick.

13   Using a 3-inch round cookie cutter, cut out circles of dough. Gather and reroll the scraps until you have 18 circles. Place each one alongside one of the $2^{1}/_{2}$-inch circles on the lined baking sheets. These 3-inch circles will serve as the top layer of crust for the pie lollipops.

14   Remove the bowl of buko filling from the fridge. Place 1 tablespoon of the filling in the center of each $2^{1}/_{2}$-inch dough circle. Insert a lollipop stick halfway up the center of the circle in the middle of the filling.

15   With your finger, coat the edges of the dough circle with egg wash. Place a 3-inch circle of dough on top and crimp the edges with a fork to seal. Repeat until all 18 pie lollipops have been assembled.

16   Brush the egg wash on top of the sealed pies with a pastry brush. Cut a small X on the top of each pie with a paring knife.

17   Bake for 15 to 20 minutes, or until the tops are golden brown. Remove the pie lollipops from the baking sheets and transfer them to a wire rack to cool completely. Serve at room temperature. Store any leftovers in an airtight container in the fridge for up to 3 days.

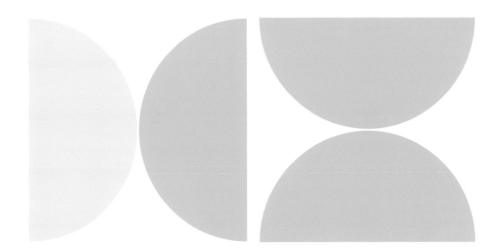

# PART IV
## Berkeley, California

*Berzerkeley*

I don't want to be a cliché, but UC Berkeley was my dream school as a kid because D.J. Tanner went there. I have this on the record in my Hello Kitty diary! UC Berkeley, or Cal for short, got its nickname since it was the first school in the University of California system before there were any others. When I was accepted to Cal in 2013, I was over the moon. The campus wasn't too far away from my parents to drive to, but I was still able to have some freedom and independence. Once I rolled up to the dorms and started my classes, I experienced a surprising culture shock. I wasn't used to seeing so many white students everywhere. It was so jarring that only about 3 percent of the students admitted to Cal during my freshman year were Filipinos, when we make up the largest Asian group in California. A majority of rich white kids who were obsessed with Greek life or played water polo resided on my floor. They were condescending, especially to me and other BIPOC in the building. I distinctly remember the frat bros harassing my friend who worked part-time in the dining commons, and how they impromptu videotaped themselves serenading him at his shift as part of a hazing challenge. Something about the way they were laughing at him, a brown student worker they never deigned to talk to before, was far from sincere. It was dehumanizing and completely unwarranted. The bubble I grew up in suddenly popped, and I was exposed to people of much higher socioeconomic status and privilege than me.

Of all the clubs that flyered around Sproul Plaza, I gravitated toward the Filipino student organizations because I felt like I had found a community where I did belong. Even when I was admitted in high school, I attended Senior Weekend with other students of color and PASS (Pilipinx Academic Student Services) members, who welcomed us with open arms. The community would host various events like mixers where they served halo-halo–shaved ice desserts piled high with tropical fruits, beans, and ube ice cream. We would dig through the layers in our red Solo cups while breaking the ice in conversation with other participants. Throughout my time at Cal, I became most involved with P4 (Partnership for Pre-Professional Pilipinxs) because I wanted to be a part of a network of Filipinos pursuing business and law careers. For one of our fundraisers, we sold homemade *pancit bihon* in the center of campus. Even the school mascot, Oski the Bear, swung by for bites of the savory stir-fried noodles jam-packed with finely chopped carrots and shredded chicken. Other P4 members also convinced me to take Filipino IA. This Tagalog language class was where I called my professor Tita Chat, sang "Bahay Kubo," and got the opportunity to relearn Tagalog with my peers for a semester.

PAA (Pilipinx American Alliance) let us freshmen join PAAmilies, where you were basically given a big who matched your personality and interests. I was paired with Ate Molly, who couldn't have been more of a perfect fit. Not only does she love the 2005 adaptation of *Pride & Prejudice*, she is a brilliant playwright and snarky older sister who has really taken me under her wing. We'd have sleepovers and she'd cook for me when I didn't have the time or wherewithal to eat a dinner that wasn't a burrito bowl from Chipotle. In May 2014, Ate Molly and I attended Ate Sydney's graduation at Cal. When the ceremony was done, they had a reception by the Campanile bell tower, where the caterers were just giving away enormous bags of free bread! I kid you not, we spent every night for a week making bread recipes *Chopped*-style. Based on the mystery ingredients Ate Molly had in the fridge, we would throw together a meal centered around our yeasted treasure. I was supremely proud of my buttery vanilla bread pudding. Every forkful was sublime and it is the blueprint for my Tsokolate Pandesal Pudding (page 224). When I started picking up my own adings, Kristina, Carissa, and Camille, I became the matriarch in a long line of wonderful ates.

During my sophomore year, I applied to get into Haas Business School within Cal. For a competitive major like business administration, you had to complete an application to be able to officially declare. Fifty percent of all applicants in each cycle weren't admitted, and I couldn't even fathom what I'd do if I got rejected. While I worked day and night on the personal essays and studying for exams, I was on the verge of a breakdown. Unlike high school, when I could turn on my mixer and bake the Advanced Placement (AP) testing stress away, it felt like there was no reprieve. My roommates, especially Yensy, who's known me since fourth grade, could tell that I was struggling. Against all odds, I persevered and got my acceptance letter. It didn't matter that I was on the verge of failing my statistics class–I did the thing! Ate Iris, who was living in the Oakland Hills at the time, even treated me to a fancy lunch to celebrate the occasion and my twentieth birthday. Chez Panisse, the renowned farm-to-table restaurant in North Berkeley, always felt so out of reach for a broke college student like me. I felt so fortunate to indulge for an afternoon, especially to have a seasonal pixie tangerine sherbet for dessert. The citrus flavor was so bright, and accentuated by candied kumquats on the side.

When I started my upper-division classes, my anxiety at Haas quadrupled. I had such intense imposter syndrome about getting into the school that I didn't feel worthy of being there. All my life, my parents taught me that I shouldn't talk back to them and I internalized a part of that as speaking up at all. Suddenly, I had to be a go-getter and raise my hand in a sea of people who I perceived were more intelligent than me. It didn't come naturally to me to think that my opinions mattered. I didn't know how to cope with this feeling of inadequacy, and it flung me down a hole where my self-confidence plummeted. For some solace, I would frequent Heavenly, my favorite Vietnamese fusion food truck on Bancroft Way and College Avenue. Before the truck sadly closed, my usual was the nem nướng, which was a grilled pork sausage

skewer fragrant with fish sauce. The woman who owned Heavenly called me "sweetie" and would give away free cups of warm *chè* chuối on Fridays. This Vietnamese warm coconut soup with tapioca pearls and bananas had a striking resemblance to *ginataang bilo-bilo*, which is my mom's favorite Filipino dessert. Through the support of my friends and many trips to Heavenly, I was able to dig myself out of my academic rut and finish my last year with a bang.

While I did receive the degrees in business administration and media studies that I had come to Berkeley for, I also got to experience four years of taking pride in my Filipino American identity. I met people who became my kuyas, ates, and adings–my chosen family. All those study dates at boba shops and walks to 10 p.m. mass on Sunday nights at Newman Hall really resonated with me. We even had an all-Filipino graduation ceremony, where I got to wear a stole with the colors of the Philippine flag. My biggest regret of my college career is that I reserved serious baking for when I'd come home to Stockton for spring break. Only my parents got to enjoy my homemade coffee macarons and cream puffs filled with a mango crème anglaise. No one from Cal got to try anything I made, and I was much too frazzled to do anything except wander around the East Bay for amazing food when school was in session.

# BROWNIES & BARS

For a student (or anyone!) on the go, brownies and bars are always convenient treats to hand to friends and pick up at the nearest coffee shop. These desserts are meant to be easy and to be shared with your loved ones.

# Turrones de Casoy MSG Brownies

### *Makes 9 squares*

My brownie preference is that I love them as close to box mix brownies as possible. I'm talking fudgy and chewy, and not cakey (emphasis on NOT). Not to yuck anyone's yum, because all your brownie choices are valid, but this recipe really caters to the fudgy brownie camp. Chopped-up Five-Spice Turrones de Casoy, a nougat recipe from the Candies chapter, and dark chocolate make it superbly decadent. A hint of MSG gives these brownies an umami boost and literally makes your mouth water. MSG, or monosodium glutamate, is a flavor enhancer that is used commonly in chips, instant ramen seasoning, and so much more. Make sure you have a glass of milk nearby when eating these brownies because each bite is so rich that you'll need something to help wash it down!

* Nonstick spray
* 6 ounces dark chocolate (60% to 72% cacao)
* 4 Five-Spice Turrones de Casoy (page 88; see Note)
* ²/₃ cup olive oil
* 2 large eggs plus 2 large egg yolks, at room temperature
* 1 teaspoon vanilla extract
* 1¹/₂ cups powdered sugar
* ¹/₂ cup packed dark brown sugar
* ³/₄ cup all-purpose flour
* ²/₃ cup unsweetened cocoa powder
* ¹/₂ teaspoon kosher salt
* ¹/₂ teaspoon MSG
* 1 teaspoon instant coffee

*Note: If you would prefer to skip the turrones de casoy, 4 single-size Snickers or Milky Way candy bars would be a good alternative.*

1   Position a rack in the middle of the oven and preheat the oven to 325°F.

2   Grease an 8 × 8-inch square pan with nonstick spray and line with parchment paper. You want enough overhang on all sides to be able to lift the baked brownie out with ease later.

3   Place the chocolate on a cutting board and coarsely chop. Transfer the chopped chocolate to a small bowl.

4   Cut each of the turrones de casoy into four equal pieces. Each piece should be 1 inch long.

5   In a large bowl, combine the olive oil, eggs, egg yolks, vanilla, and sugars. Whisk together until smooth and glossy, 2 to 3 minutes.

6   In a medium bowl, whisk together the flour, cocoa powder, kosher salt, MSG, and instant coffee.

7   Gently whisk the flour mixture into the egg yolk mixture until there are no visible streaks of flour.

8   Using a rubber spatula, fold in the chopped chocolate until evenly distributed. Pour the brownie batter into the prepared pan.

9   Stud the surface of the batter with chopped turrones de casoy before baking.

10   Bake for 40 to 45 minutes, or until a toothpick inserted into the center comes up with only a few moist crumbs. The brownie should barely pull away from the pan. Transfer the pan to a wire rack to cool completely.

11   When it's cooled, use the parchment overhang to lift the brownie out of the pan. Cut into 9 squares and serve. Store any leftovers in an airtight container at room temperature for up to 4 days.

# Corn Maja Blanca Bars

### *Makes 9 bars*

One of my favorite parts of making food is seeing that a dish can be reinvented in a vast number of ways. At its core, maja blanca is a Filipino corn and coconut milk pudding. The wide range of potential maja blanca interpretations stretches far and wide. I wanted to do more than one twist on this classic dessert besides the Malted Milk Maja Blanca with Corn Chip Crunch (page 254) in the Custards, Puddings & Chilled Desserts chapter. For this recipe, I made a layered bar with three key textural sections. At the base, we have a sweet cornmeal biscuit. The white filling is haupia, which is a Hawaiian coconut dessert that has a gelatinous texture. The tops are then dusted with freeze-dried corn powder. I hope this inspires you to take some chances with incorporating familiar flavors in new and interesting ways.

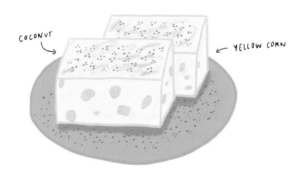

MAJA BLANCA

COCONUT

YELLOW CORN

* Nonstick spray
* ⅓ cup yellow cornmeal
* ⅔ cup all-purpose flour
* 1 teaspoon baking powder
* ½ teaspoon kosher salt
* ½ cup powdered sugar
* 8 tablespoons (1 stick) unsalted butter, cold, cut into tablespoon-size pieces

* 1 large egg, cold
* 1 teaspoon vanilla extract
* 2 (13.5-ounce) cans unsweetened, full-fat coconut milk
* ½ cup cornstarch
* ¾ cup granulated sugar
* 2 tablespoons freeze-dried corn powder

*Continued*

1   Position a rack in the middle of the oven and preheat the oven to 350°F. Grease an 8 × 8-inch square pan with nonstick spray and line with parchment paper. You want enough overhang on all sides to be able to lift the dessert out with ease later.

2   Place the cornmeal, flour, baking powder, salt, powdered sugar, butter, egg, and vanilla in a food processor. Blitz until the mixture forms a dough ball, 20 to 25 pulses.

3   Press the dough into the bottom of the lined pan in an even layer.

4   Bake for 17 to 20 minutes, or until a toothpick inserted into the center comes out clean. The edges should be golden brown. Set aside to cool on a wire rack while you work on the haupia filling.

5   In a small bowl, whisk 1 cup of the coconut milk with the cornstarch until smooth and no lumps remain.

6   Combine the remaining coconut milk and granulated sugar together in a medium saucepan. Cook over medium-high heat, stirring frequently with a rubber spatula until the mixture reaches a boil, 4 to 5 minutes. Immediately stir in the coconut milk–cornstarch mixture.

7   Reduce the heat to low and continue to cook until the mixture reaches a thick puddinglike consistency, 5 to 6 minutes.

8   Pour the haupia over the cornmeal layer. Spread in an even layer and let it cool at room temperature for 30 minutes. Cover the pan with plastic wrap and chill in the fridge for at least 2 hours.

9   Once it's done chilling, take the pan out of the fridge. Use the parchment paper overhang to remove the dessert from the pan. Cut into 9 bars.

10   Using a small sieve, dust the tops of the bars with the freeze-dried corn powder. Serve cold, and store any leftovers in the fridge in an airtight container for up to 3 days.

*Note: Once the bars are completely chilled, the haupia layer tends to come apart from the cornmeal layer. However, you can easily plop them back on after you've cut them into squares.*

# Ube Cheesecake Bars with a Sesame Cracker Crust

*Makes 6 bars*

In the early 2000s, Philadelphia Cream Cheese used to sell ready-made strawberry cheesecake bars at grocery stores. I was obsessed with them! Much to my chagrin, they were discontinued years ago. I haven't stopped thinking about these snacks, and this recipe is an ode to them. Instead of sticking to the strawberry jam, I decided to adapt the flavors to match ube cheesecake cupcakes that I made for a Filipino pop-up in September 2020. They were such a hit (my boyfriend, Jason, still asks me to make them!) that I wanted to try my hand at making a revamped version here. By hollowing out the centers of the cheesecake bars, you have a clear runway for an ube halaya filling and you get a taste of the purple yam jam with every bite. The crust is composed of Gosomi crackers, Korean sweet and salty snacks with a strong sesame flavor. Paired with ube, they perfectly complement each other.

* Nonstick spray
* 1¼ cups Gosomi cracker crumbs (from 64 crackers, about 4 packs; see Note)
* 1¼ cups sugar
* 4 tablespoons (½ stick) unsalted butter, melted
* 2 (8-ounce) cream cheese blocks, left to soften at room temperature for 1 hour
* 3 large eggs, at room temperature
* ¼ cup sour cream, at room temperature
* ¼ teaspoon kosher salt
* 1 teaspoon vanilla extract
* ¾ cup ube halaya, store-bought or homemade (see page 24)
* ¾ cup white chocolate chips
* ½ tablespoon coconut oil

*Note: If you can't find Gosomi, you can use graham crackers as an alternative.*

1   Position a rack in the middle of the oven and preheat the oven to 325°F. Line an 8 × 8-inch square pan with foil. You want enough overhang on all sides to be able to lift the dessert out with ease later. Lightly grease the surface with nonstick spray.

2   Mix together the cracker crumbs, ¼ cup of the sugar, and the butter in a medium bowl until well combined. Use the bottom of a cup to press the crumb mixture into the bottom of the pan in an even layer. Bake for 10 to 12 minutes, or until

*Continued*

lightly browned. Transfer to a wire rack to cool while you make the filling.

3    Place the softened cream cheese and the remaining 1 cup sugar in the bowl of a stand mixer fitted with the paddle attachment. Beat on medium-high speed for 1 minute. Reduce the speed to low and add the eggs one at a time, beating after each egg until it is fully incorporated into the batter. Scrape down the bottom and sides of the bowl with a rubber spatula. Add in the sour cream, salt, and vanilla until just combined, 1 to 2 minutes.

4    Pour the filling into the prepared crust. Bake for 40 to 45 minutes, or until the center has a slight wobble but the edges are set. Turn off the oven, but leave the cheesecake in there for 18 to 20 minutes with the oven door cracked open slightly. Transfer to a wire cooling rack to cool at room temperature for 30 minutes. Cover the cheesecake with plastic wrap and chill in the fridge for at least 4 hours, preferably overnight.

5    Once the cheesecake is done chilling, use the foil overhang to remove it from the pan. Divide into six equal rectangles. Using a melon baller, scoop out the centers of the cheesecake bars. Be careful not to scrape into the crust. Set the innards aside and eat as a snack. Fill each hollow center with about 2 tablespoons of the ube halaya.

6    Place the white chocolate chips and coconut oil in a small microwave-safe bowl. Microwave for 30-second intervals and mix between each round with a spoon until the chocolate has melted completely.

7    Using a spoon, drizzle the surface of the bars with chocolate. Let the chocolate harden before serving. Store any leftovers in an airtight container in the fridge for up to 5 days.

# Toasted Pinipig Marshmallow Treats

*Makes 9 squares*

I just know that Asian mothers are Costco's target demographic on the West Coast—my mother included! Whenever she'd buy us snacks in elementary school, she'd buy them in bulk there. For someone who often vetoed our requests for junk food, she was surprisingly lenient whenever we asked for Rice Krispies treats. At some point, I grew tired of the sixty-pack after getting one a day in my school lunch bag.

Now that years have gone by, I've been ready to foray back into eating marshmallow treats. I first made a batch with furikake for a Valentine's pasalubong treat box in February 2021, and now I can't fathom including a recipe without this Japanese seasoning. My homemade version benefits in texture and taste from the addition of furikake and toasted pinipig. The combination of nori, sesame seeds, salt, and kelp powder in the Trader Joe's furikake I like to use for these treats adds a salty, umami finish on top. Pinipig are pounded glutinous rice flakes that you'll commonly see in the freezer section of Filipino grocery stores. They're often used as a crispy topping for halo-halo. Since you also toast the pinipig for this recipe, they provide a nutty crunch to this dessert.

* Nonstick spray
* 1³/₄ cups frozen pinipig, thawed
* 5¹/₂ cups Rice Krispies cereal
* 6 tablespoons unsalted butter
* 1 teaspoon sesame oil
* 10 ounces marshmallows (about 6 cups), store-bought, or 1 recipe Double-Toasted Coconut Marshmallows (page 91)
* 2 tablespoons furikake

1   Line an 8 × 8-inch square pan with aluminum foil. You want enough overhang on all sides to be able to lift the dessert out with ease later. Lightly grease the surface with nonstick spray.

2   Place the pinipig in a large saucepan. Cook over low heat, stirring frequently with a rubber spatula for 10 to 12 minutes, or until golden brown and fragrant. Transfer the toasted pinipig to a large bowl, and add the Rice Krispies to the bowl. Set aside.

*Continued*

3   Add the butter and sesame oil to the large saucepan. Cook over medium-high heat until the butter is melted, 3 to 4 minutes.

4   Mix in the marshmallows and stir occasionally until they melt completely, 4 to 5 minutes. Turn off the heat and immediately add the Rice Krispies mixture. Stir until it becomes evenly coated in the melted marshmallows and butter.

5   Quickly transfer the contents of the saucepan to the prepared pan. Press it into the pan with your rubber spatula until it forms an even layer, and sprinkle all over with the furikake.

6   Wait for the mixture to cool completely before cutting into 9 squares. Store any leftovers in an airtight container at room temperature for up to 2 days.

# COOKIES

**I want to expand your horizons beyond the humble sugar cookie and pack of double-stuffed Oreos in your emergency reserve of study snacks. Cookies are a blank canvas when it comes to textures, shapes, and flavors. Ever thought of capturing the essence of sinigang (Filipino sour tamarind stew) in a cookie?**

# Rainbow Fruit Polvoron (Shortbread Cookies)

*Makes 80 cookies*

Polvoron are crumbly Filipino shortbread cookies that come in an assortment of flavors ranging from peanut to pinipig. I'm a big fan of adding freeze-dried fruits to my polvoron because they brighten the flavor of the cookies without altering their trademark powdery consistency. I always see a variety of bags of freeze-dried fruits at Trader Joe's. It's fun to bring them home, crush up the fruits, and add more color and life to any batch of cookies you make.

There are special stainless steel polvoron molders you can buy from Filipino stores, but I never see them in my neck of the woods. However, I do have a ton of fun plunger cutter shapes that do the job.

* 2 ounces assorted freeze-dried fruits (I like to use raspberry, mango, banana, etc., for a variety of flavors!)
* 1²/₃ cups all-purpose flour
* ²/₃ cup whole milk powder
* ¹/₂ cup sugar
* ¹/₄ teaspoon kosher salt
* 1¹/₄ cups (2¹/₂ sticks) unsalted butter
* 1 teaspoon vanilla extract
* Assorted gel food coloring

1   Depending on how many different flavors of freeze-dried fruits you have, divide them equally into separate plastic snack bags. Seal the bags and use a rolling pin to pulverize them. Once ground to a powder, set aside.

2   Place the flour in a large saucepan. Cook over low heat, stirring occasionally with a rubber spatula, for 10 to 12 minutes, or until the flour turns light brown and fragrant. Turn off the heat and transfer the toasted flour to a large bowl.

3   Add the whole milk powder, sugar, and salt to the bowl. Whisk together until all of the ingredients are well combined.

4   Place the butter in a medium microwave-safe bowl and microwave in 30-second intervals until completely melted. Stir in the vanilla. While still warm, add the butter mixture to the flour mixture.

*Continued*

5    Divide the crumbly polvoron dough into different bowls, based on the number of flavors you want to make.

6    Mix a freeze-dried fruit into each bowl by hand. Add drops of your choice of gel food coloring to tint the different dough flavors. It helps to wear gloves during this process so you don't stain your hands.

7    Line two baking sheets with parchment paper. Form desired polvoron shapes by packing the mixture into your polvoron molder or plunger cutter. It's best to shape the polvoron when the dough is still warm, so feel free to pop your bowl in the microwave for 10 to 15 seconds if you feel like the mixture has gotten cold. Be careful not to press the mixture in too hard or it will get stuck in the mold. Release each shaped polvoron onto the prepared baked sheets.

8    Once you're done shaping each polvoron, place the baking sheets in the fridge and chill for at least 1 hour to allow the polvoron to set.

9    After chilling, you can wrap each one individually in tissue paper or cellophane. Alternatively, you can skip that step and serve the polvoron on a plate. Store any leftovers in an airtight container at room temperature for up to 1 week.

# Adobo Chocolate Chip Cookies

*Makes 22 cookies*

Chicken adobo stewed in soy sauce and vinegar was always the dinner my parents cooked for us when they needed to fix up a quick but delicious meal. For my signature chocolate chip cookie recipe, I wanted to incorporate all of adobo's nuanced and comforting flavors. I am a big fan of incorporating savory into my desserts, and this recipe is no exception. Miso chocolate chip cookies have been everywhere lately, and I thought that soy sauce acts as an excellent alternative source of salt. For an acid to help with activating the baking soda, apple cider vinegar is mixed into the dough.

To add a hint of herbal flavor, I steep a couple bay leaves in the butter while it's browning. Last but not least, toasted pink peppercorns adorn the cookies. When you take a bite with some of the chopped dark chocolate, they help accentuate the fruitier, more floral notes of the chocolate while adding a hint of spice. As a kid, I'd wince every time I took a bite of a whole black peppercorn while eating adobo. For these cookies, I opted for pink peppercorns specifically since they're milder and less harsh on the tongue.

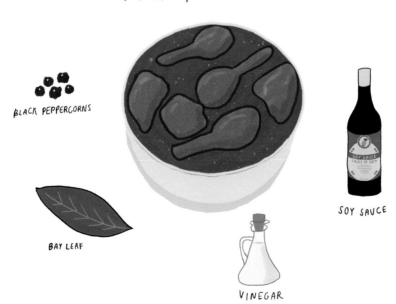

KEY SAVORY ADOBO INGREDIENTS

BLACK PEPPERCORNS

BAY LEAF

VINEGAR

SOY SAUCE

*Continued*

- ½ pound (2 sticks) unsalted butter
- 2 fresh bay leaves (or 4 dried bay leaves)
- I cup packed dark brown sugar
- ¾ cup granulated sugar
- I large egg plus I large egg yolk, at room temperature
- ¼ cup soy sauce (regular sodium)
- I teaspoon apple cider vinegar
- 2 teaspoons vanilla extract
- 2¼ cups all-purpose flour
- I teaspoon baking soda
- IO ounces dark chocolate (60% to 72% cacao), coarsely chopped
- I tablespoon pink peppercorns
- Flaky sea salt, for garnish

1    Place the butter and bay leaves in a medium saucepan. Cook over medium-low heat, stirring frequently with a rubber spatula until the butter melts and gets golden brown, 5 to 7 minutes. Pour the brown butter into a large bowl and discard the bay leaves. Set aside until cool enough to touch, about IO minutes.

2    Add both sugars to the brown butter and whisk by hand until well combined. Mix in the egg, egg yolk, soy sauce, apple cider vinegar, and vanilla.

3    In a separate medium bowl, mix together the flour and baking soda until the baking soda is evenly distributed.

4    Gently whisk the flour mixture into the butter mixture until no flour streaks remain.

5    With a rubber spatula, fold in the chocolate.

6    Cover the bowl with plastic wrap or a lid and chill the dough in the fridge for at least

30 minutes. Ideally, you'd want to let it rest overnight to allow more time for the flavors to meld. After an overnight rest, the cookies have an intense caramel flavor once baked. If you're resting the dough overnight, just make sure you let the dough sit at room temperature for 30 minutes to make it easier to scoop into balls.

7    Position a rack in the middle of the oven and preheat the oven to 350°F. Line two baking sheets with silicone mats.

8    Using a 3-tablespoon cookie scoop, portion the dough into balls. Place six dough balls on one of the prepared baking sheets, making sure to leave at least 2 inches of space between the balls. Place the bowl of remaining cookie dough back in the fridge until the first sheet is done baking.

9    In a small skillet, toast the pink peppercorns on low heat until they start to smell fragrant, 2 to 3 minutes. Grind the peppercorns with a mortar and pestle until they're coarsely crushed.

10   Sprinkle some of the crushed pink peppercorns and flaky sea salt on top of the dough balls before popping the baking sheet into the oven.

11   Bake for IO to I2 minutes, or until the edges of the cookies are golden brown. Before taking the cookies out of the oven, drop the sheet against the oven rack a couple times at a height of about 4 to 5 inches to create outer ripples in the cookies. Transfer the baking sheet to a wire rack to cool completely.

12   Repeat the process with the remaining cookie dough and the other lined baking sheet until all the dough is baked.

# Red Velvet Sylvanas
## (Cashew Meringue Sandwich Cookies)

*Makes 30 sandwich cookies*

For the first eighteen years of my existence, I thought that chain restaurants were the pinnacle of fine dining. Casual dining establishments were the places to be in suburbia. When I first had the red velvet cake at California Pizza Kitchen, I thought it was the most incredible dessert I had ever tasted. While anyone from the South will tell you that CPK is not really considered a go-to red velvet purveyor, it turned me into a red velvet lifer.

Sylvanas, or silvanas, are Filipino cashew meringue sandwich cookies filled with buttercream. Although I didn't have sylvanas as often as CPK cake, I was always eager to buy them. My parents would tell me not to bother trying them since they thought that the French buttercream inside tasted like a stick of butter, but that just made me want to eat the treats more! For a red velvet rendition, I added a touch of red food coloring and cocoa powder to the dacquoise. Instead of a French buttercream, I opted for tangy cream cheese frosting that makes the dessert not too sweet and hopefully more appealing to my parents. I like to eat these sylvanas after dinner with a glass of milk or even as a refreshing snack anytime, since I just keep them in my freezer.

## Dacquoise

* 1¾ cups raw cashews
* 2 tablespoons unsweetened cocoa powder
* 6 large egg whites, at room temperature
* ½ teaspoon cream of tartar
* ¾ cup granulated sugar
* 4 to 6 drops red gel food coloring

## Cream Cheese Frosting

* 2 (8-ounce) blocks cream cheese, left to soften at room temperature for 1 hour
* ½ pound (2 sticks) unsalted butter, at room temperature

* 2 cups powdered sugar, sifted
* 1 teaspoon vanilla extract
* ¾ teaspoon kosher salt

## Topping

* 1½ cups graham cracker crumbs (from about 12 graham cracker sheets)
* 6 to 8 drops red gel food coloring

*Continued*

## Dacquoise

**1**  Position a rack in the middle of the oven and preheat the oven to 300°F. Line two baking sheets with silicone mats.

**2**  Place the raw cashews in a large saucepan over medium-high heat. Stir the cashews frequently with a wooden spoon for 4 to 6 minutes, or until lightly browned and fragrant. Turn off the heat.

**3**  Pour the toasted cashews into a food processor. Pulse until the cashews turn into fine crumbs, 15 to 18 pulses. Reserve ³/₄ cup of the toasted cashew crumbs for the topping in a medium bowl.

**4**  Whisk the remaining toasted cashew crumbs with the cocoa powder in a small bowl. Set aside.

**5**  In a large bowl, beat the egg whites and cream of tartar with an electric hand mixer on medium-high speed until soft peaks form, 1 to 2 minutes. Gradually add the sugar, 1 tablespoon at a time, until stiff peaks form, 2 to 3 minutes.

**6**  Add the red gel food coloring and mix on medium-high speed for another 1 to 2 minutes, or until the mixture is a homogenous light red color.

**7**  In three batches, gently fold the cashew-cocoa powder mixture into the meringue with a rubber spatula. Try to avoid deflating the meringue in the folding process.

**8**  Transfer your cashew meringue to a piping bag fitted with a large round tip. Pipe 30 circles that are 2 inches wide and at least ¹/₂ inch apart on each lined baking sheet.

**9**  Dampen your finger with a little water and gently flatten any peaks that form on the tops of the meringues.

**10**  Bake one sheet at a time for 25 to 30 minutes, or until the tops of the meringue cookies are set. They puff up a bit in the oven, but they will shrink in height as they cool. Allow the meringue cookies to cool on the baking sheets for 15 minutes before peeling them off the silicone mats and transferring them to a wire rack to cool completely.

## Cream Cheese Frosting

**11**  Place the softened cream cheese and butter in the bowl of a stand mixer fitted with the paddle attachment. Beat together on medium-high speed until well combined, about 1 minute.

**12**  Adjust the mixer to the lowest speed and gradually add in the powdered sugar, vanilla, and salt. Once the ingredients have all been added, increase the speed to medium-high. Cream until light and fluffy, 1 to 2 minutes.

**13**  Scrape down the sides and bottom of the bowl with a rubber spatula. Increase the speed to medium-high again and beat for an additional 1 to 2 minutes to ensure the frosting ingredients are evenly incorporated. Set aside.

## Topping

**14**  Mix the graham cracker and the reserved roasted cashew crumbs together in the medium bowl until well combined.

**15**  In a small bowl, whisk 3 tablespoons water and the red gel food coloring until the color is homogenous.

16  Pour the water mixture over the graham cracker mixture. Toss with your hands until all the crumbs are bright red and the color is evenly distributed. Feel free to wear gloves for this part if you don't want to temporarily stain your fingertips.

## Assembly

17  Line up each meringue cookie half with a corresponding cookie to make a matching pair.

18  Turn half of the cookies over and spread an even layer of the frosting over the cookie. Gently press the cookie counterpart on top of the frosted layer. After gently squeezing them together, smooth out any excess of frosting that reaches past the outer edges of the cookie sandwich.

19  Using an offset spatula, coat each cookie sandwich with a thin layer of frosting on the top and bottom. Immediately roll all over in the topping mixture.

20  Place the finished sylvanas on the lined baking sheets and freeze for at least 30 minutes before transferring them to an airtight container where you can stack them. Store the sylvanas in the freezer for up to 2 weeks and serve cold.

# Matamis na Bao Alfajores
## (Coconut Jam Shortbread Sandwich Cookies)

*Makes 22 sandwich cookies*

Alfajores are popular South American shortbread sandwich cookies filled with dulce de leche. When I was living in Berkeley during my undergrad years, I remember having alfajores for the first time after getting brunch at a restaurant called 900 Grayson. I went there for the *Hobbit*-themed menu, but they had packaged alfajores for sale at the register too, and I couldn't resist snagging one. There's such a delicate balance of the crumbly cookie paired with a scrumptious filling of caramelized condensed milk. Since alfajores can be rolled in unsweetened shredded coconut, I thought to swap the dulce de leche with matamis na bao for a more intense coconut experience. While there is a recipe for matamis na bao in the Jams, Syrups & Toppings chapter, you can also buy jars of this coconut jam at your local Filipino grocery store. No matter how you make alfajores, it's a luxurious experience eating them.

* 1½ cups all-purpose flour, plus more for dusting
* 1 cup cornstarch
* ½ teaspoon kosher salt
* ¾ cup plus 2 tablespoons powdered sugar
* ½ pound (2 sticks) unsalted butter, at room temperature
* 1 teaspoon vanilla extract
* 1 large egg plus 1 large egg yolk, at room temperature
* 1¼ cups plus 2 tablespoons matamis na bao, homemade (page 26) or store-bought
* ¼ cup unsweetened shredded coconut, for rolling

1   Whisk together the all-purpose flour, cornstarch, salt, and ¾ cup of the powdered sugar in a medium bowl. Set aside.

2   Place the butter and vanilla in the bowl of a stand mixer fitted with the paddle attachment. Beat on medium-high speed until well combined, 1 to 2 minutes. With the mixer still running, add the egg and the egg yolk one at a time. After each addition, make sure to beat until the mixture is well combined and the egg is fully incorporated. Adjust the mixer to the lowest speed and gradually stir in the flour mixture until it forms a dough and there are no flour streaks remaining, 1 to 2 minutes.

3   Take out the dough with a rubber spatula and flatten into a 2-inch-thick disc. Wrap in plastic

*Continued*

wrap and place it in the fridge to rest for at least 1 hour.

4    Position a rack in the middle of the oven and preheat the oven to 350°F. Line two baking sheets with silicone mats.

5    Lightly flour a rolling pin and your work surface. Take the chilled cookie dough out of the fridge and plop it on your work surface. Roll the dough out about $\frac{1}{4}$ inch thick. Using a $2\frac{1}{4}$-inch scalloped round cookie cutter, cut out rounds of dough and place on the lined baking sheets. Gather and reroll the scraps until you have a total of 44 rounds.

6    Using a fork, prick the center of each cookie before popping one baking sheet in the oven. Place the other baking sheet in the fridge until the first batch is done baking. Bake for 11 to 13 minutes, or until the cookies are just set. They shouldn't have any color on them. Allow to cool on the baking sheet for 5 minutes, then transfer to a wire cooling rack. Repeat with the second baking sheet.

7    When the cookies have completely cooled, line up each cookie with a corresponding cookie to make a matching pair. Flip half of them upside down and scoop 1 tablespoon of matamis na bao on the surface of each flipped cookie. Place the cookie counterpart on top of each matamis na bao layer. Gently squeeze each cookie sandwich together until the jam reaches the edge of the cookie.

8    Place the unsweetened shredded coconut in a small bowl. Roll the cookie sides in the coconut.

9    With a small sieve, sprinkle the tops of the alfajores with the remaining 2 tablespoons powdered sugar. Store the alfajores in an airtight container at room temperature for up to 3 days.

# Kare-Kare Cookies

*Makes 36 cookies*

For these cookies, I wanted to interpret one of my favorite savory dishes in a sweet way. Kare-kare is traditionally a peanut butter stew that is served with heaps of white rice and bagoong. It's time-consuming and not something you just throw together. It takes hours to tenderize oxtail and get the stew right, and it really is a labor of love to be made for a special occasion. Whenever I'd come home from college on winter break, my dad would cook kare-kare for me since I missed it so much.

Creamy peanut butter flavors these chewy, thick cookies. The dough is rolled in an annatto-sugar mixture before baking to give them a burnt-orange color. The centers of these cookies are filled with spicy bagoong caramels, which get slightly melted in the oven so you get a taste of sweet, shrimpy goodness with every bite.

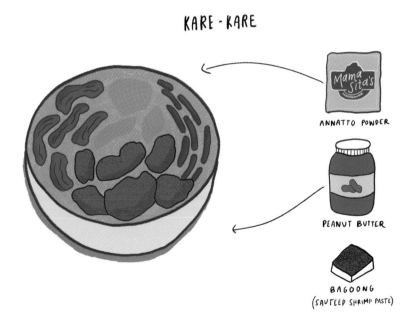

KARE-KARE

ANNATTO POWDER

PEANUT BUTTER

BAGOONG
(SAUTEED SHRIMP PASTE)

*Continued*

- **8 tablespoons (I stick) unsalted butter, at room temperature**
- **1/2 cup creamy peanut butter**
- **I cup packed dark brown sugar**
- **I large egg plus I large egg yolk, at room temperature**
- **I teaspoon vanilla extract**
- **1 1/4 cups all-purpose flour**
- **3/4 teaspoon baking soda**
- **1/2 teaspoon baking powder**
- **1/2 teaspoon kosher salt**
- **1/4 cup granulated sugar**
- **2 teaspoons annatto powder**
- **36 Spicy Bagoong Caramels (page 86)**

1   Position an oven rack in the middle of the oven and preheat the oven to 350°F. Line two baking sheets with silicone mats and set aside.

2   Place the butter, peanut butter, and brown sugar in the bowl of a stand mixer fitted with the paddle attachment. Beat together on medium-high speed until light and fluffy, 3 to 4 minutes.

3   Mix in the egg, egg yolk, and vanilla until the mixture is well combined. Scrape down the sides and bottom of the bowl with a rubber spatula.

4   In a separate medium bowl, whisk together the flour, baking soda, baking powder, and salt until well combined.

5   Adjust the mixer to the lowest speed and gradually stir in the flour mixture until it forms a dough and there are little to no flour streaks.

6   In a small bowl, mix together the granulated sugar and annatto powder.

7   Using a I-tablespoon cookie scoop, portion the dough into 18 balls and roll them twice in the sugar mixture. Place the dough balls on one of the prepared baking sheets, making sure to leave at least 1 1/2 inches of space between the balls.

8   Bake for 6 minutes. Take the baking sheet out of the oven and insert a spicy bagoong caramel in the center of each cookie. Immediately return the sheet to the oven and bake for an additional 3 to 4 minutes, or until the edges of the cookies are golden brown. Before taking the cookies out of the oven, drop the sheet against the oven rack a couple times at a height of about 4 to 5 inches to create outer ripples in the cookies. Transfer the baking sheet to a wire rack to cool completely.

9   Repeat the process with the remaining cookie dough and the other lined baking sheet until all the dough is baked. Store any leftovers in an airtight container at room temperature for up to 3 days.

# Sampalok Tajín Snickerdoodles

*Makes 28 cookies*

I think it's hilarious that the Tajín bottle has a disclaimer on it that reads "This Is Not a Candy." When I was growing up in Stockton, us kids were eating it like Lucas, a sweet and sour powder kind of like the Mexican candy equivalent of the topping for Baby Bottle Pops or Fun Dip. Early on, my palate gained an affinity for the chili-lime taste of Tajín and many Mexican candies. At the same time that I got into Tajín, I remember enjoying the sweets in the pasalubong boxes my relatives would bring back from the Philippines. In some shipments, there would be shiny cellophane wrappers of tamarind candy. The tart fruit came in pods like dark brown peas. Salted and sometimes spicy, the sugar-coated sampalok was a favorite of mine. Marrying tamarind powder and Tajín in a snickerdoodle cookie seems like something eight-year-old me would love. It even reminds me of sinigang, my favorite sour tamarind Filipino stew (I like to add jalapeños to my broth for extra heat!).

PORK SINIGANG

GREEN BEANS

TOMATO

MUSTARD GREENS

TARO

JALAPENO

OKRA

PORK SPARE RIBS

*Continued*

- ½ pound (2 sticks) unsalted butter, at room temperature
- 1½ cups plus 2 tablespoons granulated sugar
- ¼ cup packed dark brown sugar
- 1 large egg plus 1 large egg yolk, at room temperature
- 1 teaspoon vanilla extract
- 2½ cups all-purpose flour
- 2 teaspoons cream of tartar
- 1 teaspoon baking soda
- ½ teaspoon kosher salt
- 3 tablespoons tamarind powder
- 2 tablespoons Tajín

1   Position a rack in the middle of the oven and preheat the oven to 350°F. Line two baking sheets with silicone mats and set aside.

2   Place the butter, 1¼ cups of the granulated sugar, and the brown sugar in the bowl of a stand mixer fitted with the paddle attachment. Beat together on medium-high speed until light and fluffy, 3 to 4 minutes. Mix in the egg, egg yolk, and vanilla until the mixture is well combined. Scrape down the sides and bottom of the bowl with a rubber spatula.

3   In a separate medium bowl, whisk the flour, cream of tartar, baking soda, and salt until well combined. Adjust the mixer to the lowest speed and gradually stir in the flour mixture until it forms a dough and there are little to no flour streaks.

4   In a small bowl, mix together the remaining ¼ cup plus 2 tablespoons granulated sugar, the tamarind powder, and Tajín. Using a 2-tablespoon cookie scoop, portion the dough into balls and roll them twice in the sugar mixture. Place six

dough balls on one of the prepared baking sheets, making sure to leave at least 2 inches of space between the balls.

5   Bake for 10 to 12 minutes, or until the edges of the cookies are golden brown. Before taking the cookies out of the oven, drop the sheet against the oven rack a couple times at a height of about 4 to 5 inches to create outer ripples in the cookies. Transfer the baking sheet to a wire rack to cool completely.

6   Repeat the process with the remaining cookie dough and the other lined baking sheet until all the dough is baked. Store any leftovers in an airtight container at room temperature for up to 3 days.

# Filipino Flag Red, Blue, Yellow & White Cookies

*Makes 12 cookies*

When I first moved to New York, I couldn't help but notice black and white cookies in every deli. Considering the fact that they are actually just large drop cakes topped with icing, the "cookie" title is a bit baffling, but I absolutely love them. The contrast in icing colors is so striking that I thought I'd make a version that is a nod to the colors of the Filipino flag. The tinted halves are flavored with a jasmine extract, which represents the national flower of the Philippines—the sampaguita. The jasmine extract makes the cookies sweet and fragrant, and gives them a light, floral taste.

## Cookies

* 12 tablespoons (1½ sticks) unsalted butter, at room temperature
* I cup granulated sugar
* I large egg plus I large egg yolk, at room temperature
* ½ cup buttermilk, at room temperature
* 2 teaspoons vanilla extract
* 1¾ cups all-purpose flour
* ½ teaspoon kosher salt
* ½ teaspoon baking powder
* ¼ teaspoon baking soda

## Icing

* 2½ cups powdered sugar, sifted
* I tablespoon plus ¾ teaspoon light corn syrup
* ¾ cup plus ½ teaspoon heavy cream
* ¼ teaspoon jasmine extract
* ¼ teaspoon vanilla extract
* 2 to 4 drops red gel food coloring
* 2 to 4 drops blue gel food coloring
* 2 to 4 drops yellow food coloring

## Cookies

1   Position a rack in the middle of the oven and preheat the oven to 350°F. Line two baking sheets with silicone mats and set aside.

2   Place the butter and sugar in the bowl of a stand mixer fitted with the paddle attachment. Cream on medium-high speed until light and fluffy, 3 to 4 minutes. Add in the egg and egg yolk one at a time. Scrape down the bottom and sides of the bowl with a rubber spatula. Mix on medium-high speed until well combined and smooth. Stir together the buttermilk and vanilla in a small measuring cup.

3   Whisk the flour, salt, baking powder, and baking soda in a medium bowl. Adjust the mixer to

*Continued*

the lowest speed. Starting with the flour mixture, add it to the mixer in three batches, alternating with the buttermilk mixture, until just combined. Scrape down the bottom and sides of the bowl, and give the mixture a couple folds to ensure that everything is evenly incorporated.

4    Using a $\frac{1}{4}$-cup ice cream scoop, scoop six balls of batter per lined baking sheet. Make sure to space them about $3\frac{1}{2}$ to 4 inches apart since they spread a lot while baking.

5    Bake one sheet at a time for 15 to 17 minutes, or until a toothpick inserted in the center of one comes out clean and the edges are golden brown. Transfer the baking sheet to a wire rack to cool completely. Repeat the baking process for the remaining cookies.

## Icing

6    In a large bowl, whisk together the powdered sugar, corn syrup, and heavy cream until smooth. Transfer half of the plain icing to a medium bowl. Add the jasmine extract to the remaining icing that's in the large bowl. Divide equally into 3 separate small bowls.

7    To the plain icing, stir in the vanilla. To one of the small bowls, stir in the red gel food coloring. To the second small bowl, stir in the blue gel food coloring. To the last small bowl, stir in the yellow gel food coloring.

## Assembly

8    Peel the cooled cookies off the silicone mats and flip them so that they are flat side up.

9    Cover half of each of the cookies with a thin layer of vanilla icing, using an offset spatula lightly pressed at the center as a guide for a clean line. Set them on a wire rack for the icing to set, about 15 minutes.

10    Cover the remaining half of each cookie with the tinted jasmine icing. You should have four of each colorway. Let the icing completely harden, at least 1 hour, before serving. Store any leftovers in an airtight container at room temperature for up to 3 days.

# Lengua de Gato and Ganache Sandwich Cookies

*Makes 15 sandwich cookies*

Lengua de gato are long, crisp cookies that get their name from sharing a resemblance with a cat's tongue. They are sought-after pasalubong, especially from Baguio City. They've always reminded me of Pepperidge Farm's Milanos but without the chocolate. However, I am a chocolate fiend, so I chose to turn lengua de gato into sandwich cookies bound together by ganache. They're delightful with a cup of milk, and even though these homemade Milanos soften overnight, they're still tasty the next day.

* 8 tablespoons (1 stick) unsalted butter, at room temperature
* ½ cup sugar
* 2 large egg whites, at room temperature
* ¾ teaspoon vanilla extract
* 1 cup all-purpose flour
* ½ teaspoon kosher salt
* 3 ounces dark chocolate (60% to 72% cacao), coarsely chopped
* ¼ cup plus 2 tablespoons heavy cream

1  Position a rack in the middle of the oven and preheat the oven to 350°F. Line two baking sheets with silicone mats and set aside.

2  Place the butter and sugar in the bowl of a stand mixer fitted with the paddle attachment. Cream on medium-high speed until light and fluffy, 3 to 4 minutes. Mix in one egg white at a time, and then add in the vanilla. Scrape down the bottom and sides of the bowl with a rubber spatula. Adjust the speed of the mixer to low. Gradually stir in the flour and salt until just incorporated. Turn off the mixer and give the batter a couple of folds before transferring to a piping bag fitted with a large round tip.

3  Pipe 3-inch logs onto the lined baking sheets, spacing the logs at least 2 inches apart from one another. Using your finger dampened with some water, lightly press down any tails or peaks from the ends of the logs so they're nice and smooth.

*Continued*

4   Bake for 10 to 12 minutes, or until just the edges are golden brown and the cookies are set. Let them sit on the sheet for 5 minutes before transferring to a wire rack to cool completely. Once cooled, pair each cookie with one that matches in size. Flip half of the cookies over, so they're flat side up.

5   Place the chopped chocolate in a small microwave-safe bowl. Heat the cream in a small saucepan over low heat. Cook until it reaches a simmer, 2 to 3 minutes. Pour the cream over the chocolate and let the mixture sit for 2 to 3 minutes. Using a rubber spatula, gently stir until it forms a smooth ganache. If there are some stubborn bits of chocolate that won't melt, microwave the bowl in 10-second intervals and stir until completely melted.

6   Take one cookie that is flat side up and evenly spread a thin layer of ganache onto it, using an offset spatula, about $1/2$ tablespoon of ganache per cookie. Place the other cookie half on top and gently press them together to form a sandwich. Repeat with the rest of the cookies. Store any leftovers in an airtight container at room temperature for up to 2 days.

# Milk Chocolate Rugelach

*Makes 40 rugelach*

It's a rite of passage to go into Zabar's on the Upper West Side and grab a tub of whitefish salad. I trekked over there for the first time in 2019 to try their whitefish salad and get a gift for my friend Amy, and I was mesmerized by everything you could buy at the famous store. It was the freshly baked rugelach in the bakery section that caught my eye first. It must have been the spiral design of their rugelach that reminded me of a beloved Filipino chocolate called Curly Tops. Curly Tops taste like Hershey's milk chocolate, and are heavenly chopped up between layers of rugelach pastry.

* 1/2 pound (2 sticks) unsalted butter, cold, cut into tablespoon-size pieces
* I (8-ounce) cream cheese block, cold, cut into tablespoon-size pieces
* 2 tablespoons sour cream, cold
* 2 1/4 cups all-purpose flour, plus more for dusting
* 2 tablespoons granulated sugar
* 1/2 teaspoon kosher salt
* 1/4 cup apricot preserves
* 6 ounces Curly Tops chocolate, finely chopped
* 2 large egg yolks, at room temperature
* I tablespoon whole milk, at room temperature
* Sparkling sugar, for topping

1   Place the butter, cream cheese, sour cream, flour, sugar, and salt in a food processor. Blitz until the mixture forms a dough ball, 50 to 55 pulses. Gather the dough and divide into four equal portions. Shape each portion into a small rectangle and wrap in plastic wrap. Transfer to the fridge to chill for at least I hour.

2   Lightly flour a rolling pin and your work surface. Take one of the dough rectangles and plop it on your work surface. Roll dough out into a 6 × 12 1/2-inch rectangle. Make sure to pick up the dough and occasionally sprinkle some flour between rolls, so it doesn't stick.

3   Using a rubber spatula, evenly coat the surface with I tablespoon of the apricot preserves. Then, sprinkle 1 1/2 ounces of chopped Curly Tops in an even layer over the preserves. Starting from one of the long ends, roll into a tight log. Place on a baking sheet lined with a silicone mat, seam side down. Repeat the process with the rest of the dough. Once you have four logs evenly spaced

*Continued*

apart on the sheet, transfer to a freezer to chill for 30 minutes.

4   While the rugelach logs are freezing, position a rack in the middle of the oven and preheat the oven to 350°F.

5   In a small bowl, whisk together the egg yolks and milk until well combined. Set aside.

6   Once the rugelach logs are done chilling, take them out and make cuts halfway through the logs every 1¼ inches along the long side of the logs. You should end up with ten portions per log.

7   Using a pastry brush, coat the surface of each log with the egg wash. Sprinkle each log with sparkling sugar. Bake for 20 minutes and then rotate the baking sheet. Bake for an additional 25 to 30 minutes, or until the rugelach logs are golden brown. Some chocolate leakage is normal, and you can easily cut off those parts. Remove from the oven and let the logs cool on the baking sheet on top of a wire rack for 20 minutes.

8   Transfer the logs to a cutting board and slice all the way through the initial cuts. Place the rugelach on a wire rack to cool completely. Store any leftovers in an airtight container at room temperature for up to 3 days.

# Stamped Calamansi-Fish Sauce Shortbread

*Makes 40 cookies*

You can probably tell by now that I don't shy away from funky flavor combinations. When used in the right amounts, fermented and salty elements don't overpower the other ingredients in a dessert! Whether it's soy sauce in chocolate chip cookies or bagoong in caramels, these elements help to balance the sweetness of desserts. I remember my auntie Rina used to dip apple slices in patis, or fish sauce, so I've never been a stranger to pairing the condiment with fruit. With these shortbread cookies, the hint of patis in the glaze really amplifies the lemon-lime notes of the calamansi.

* ½ pound (2 sticks) unsalted butter, at room temperature
* 1½ cups powdered sugar
* 1 large egg plus 1 large egg yolk, at room temperature
* 1 teaspoon vanilla extract
* 2½ cups all-purpose flour, plus more for dusting
* ½ teaspoon kosher salt
* 1½ tablespoons frozen calamansi juice, thawed
* Zest of 1 lime
* ½ teaspoon patis or fish sauce

1   Place the butter and ¾ cup of the powdered sugar in the bowl of a stand mixer fitted with the paddle attachment. Cream on medium-high speed until light and fluffy, 3 to 4 minutes.

2   Mix in the egg and egg yolk one at a time. After each addition, make sure to beat until the mixture is well combined and the egg is fully incorporated. Add in the vanilla. Scrape down the bottom and sides of the bowl with a rubber spatula.

3   Adjust the speed of the mixer to low. Gradually stir in the flour and salt until just incorporated. Turn off the mixer and give the dough a couple of folds. Split the dough in half and wrap each dough ball in plastic wrap. Let the dough chill for at least 1 hour in the fridge.

*Continued*

4   Line two baking sheets with silicone mats. Lightly flour a rolling pin and your work surface. Take one of the dough balls and plop it on your work surface. Roll dough out until it's ¼ inch thick. Make sure to pick up the dough and occasionally sprinkle some flour between rolls, so it doesn't stick.

5   Using a scallop design cookie stamp or a meat tenderizer, press all over the dough until it's ⅛ inch thick and there are visible impressions on it. Take a 3-inch fish-shaped cookie cutter and cut out shapes. Place them on one of the prepared baking sheets, spacing them at least 1 inch apart. Gather and reroll the scraps until you have a total of 20 fish cookies. Repeat this process with the other ball of dough and place them on a second baking sheet lined with a silicone mat. Transfer the baking sheets to the freezer to chill for at least 30 minutes.

6   While the shaped cookie dough is chilling, position a rack in the middle of the oven and preheat the oven to 350°F.

7   Take one baking sheet out of the freezer and place it in the oven. Bake the cookies for 12 to 14 minutes, or until golden brown. Transfer the cookies to a wire rack to cool completely. Repeat the baking process with the second baking sheet.

8   Using a large sieve, sift the remaining ¾ cup powdered sugar into a medium bowl. Whisk the calamansi juice, lime zest, and patis with the sugar until it becomes a smooth glaze. Using a pastry brush, coat the surface of each cooled cookie with the glaze. Let the glaze harden for at least 30 minutes before serving the cookies. Store any leftovers in an airtight container at room temperature for up to 5 days.

# Lemon Sunshine Uraro Cookies

*Makes 44 cookies*

In December 2021, my friend Madeline had a pop-up space in Williamsburg for her sustainable fashion company, Sense of Shelf. She invited me to host an event there, so I chose to do a holiday cookie swap. It was exciting to see some new and familiar faces, and to try everyone's bakes. My boyfriend's best friend, Stephen, really pulled out all the stops with his Christmas spritz cookies. He bought a cookie press specifically for this occasion! He never really bakes, and it was wholesome to see him accomplish making his mom's recipe.

It inspired me to get my own cookie press for creating gluten-free uraro cookies. These very delicate cookies, made with arrowroot flour, are a specialty from Southern Luzon in the Philippines. They melt in your mouth and taste wonderful with the vibrant flavor of lemon. With a cookie press, you place the uraro dough inside a canister and there is a patterned disc at the bottom that the cookie is extruded through. Different patterns in the shape of trees, flowers, teddy bears, hearts, and more are included in a set. You can purchase a cookie press online or at specialty kitchenware stores for an affordable price. After baking the cookies, just be careful when transporting them. Since they're already crumbly to begin with, they are fragile and have a tendency to break apart.

* 1½ cups arrowroot flour
* 1¼ teaspoons baking powder
* ¼ teaspoon kosher salt
* ½ cup powdered sugar
* 2 large egg yolks, cold
* 8 tablespoons (1 stick) unsalted butter, cold, cut into tablespoon-size pieces
* Zest of 1 lemon
* Pastel nonpareils, for decoration

1   Position a rack in the middle of the oven and preheat the oven to 350°F.

2   Place the arrowroot flour, baking powder, salt, sugar, egg yolks, butter, and lemon zest in a food processor. Blitz until the mixture turns into a dough that clumps together and has the texture of mashed potatoes, 35 to 40 pulses.

3   Follow the directions of your cookie press to fit it with a flower-shaped die. Fill the cookie press canister with the dough. You should have enough dough to fill it up for two rounds of pressing.

*Continued*

4   Press the cookie dough onto an unlined baking sheet, spacing the cookies about 1¹/₂ to 2 inches apart. Sprinkle the flowers with nonpareils.

5   Bake for 12 to 15 minutes, until the edges turn golden brown. Take the sheet out of the oven, and let the cookies sit on the sheet for 10 minutes before carefully transferring them to a wire rack to cool completely. Make sure to use your hands, not a spatula, to lift them, because they are fragile cookies. Repeat the baking process with the other half of the dough. Store any leftovers in an airtight container at room temperature for up to 5 days.

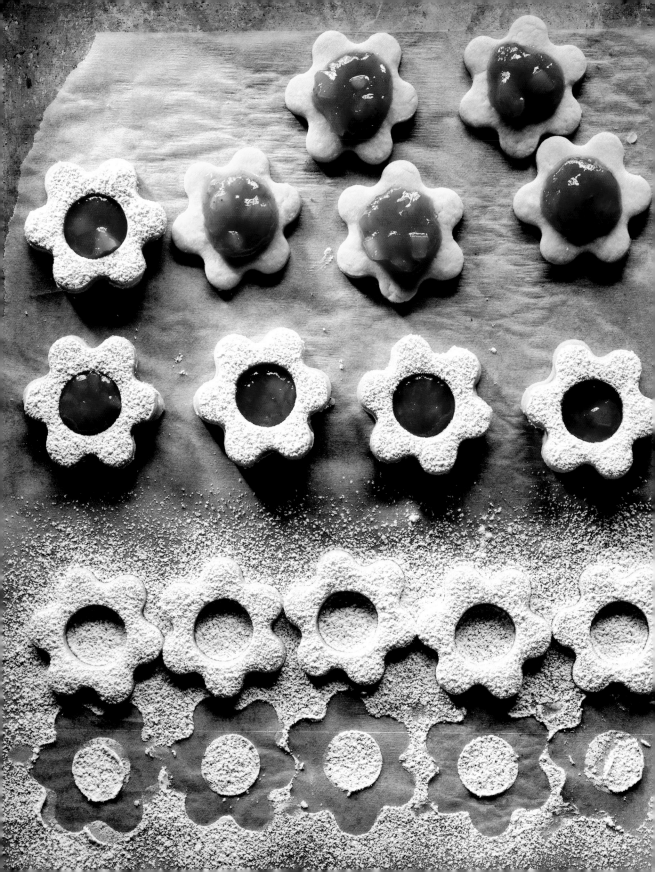

# Turon Linzer Cookies

*Makes about 60 sandwich cookies*

When I made a Christmas cookie tin for another round of pasalubong treat boxes in 2020, I had two realizations that winter: One person should never make over a thousand cookies, and that these turon linzer cookies were my favorite of the bunch. Turon is a Filipino snack that is made up of saba banana, brown sugar, and jackfruit deep-fried in a spring roll wrapper, and then coated in a caramel glaze. Linzer cookies are Austrian sandwich cookies that traditionally showcase a raspberry jam that you can see through a hole stamped out of the top cookie layer. My turon linzer cookies, a marriage of these two desserts, are composed of shortbread sandwich cookies filled with a layer of caramelized banana and jackfruit jam that taste just like tiny morsels of turon. Since I have a gigantic fear of getting oil burns, I definitely prefer making these cookies to having to be on fryer duty.

* ½ pound (2 sticks) unsalted butter, at room temperature
* ¾ cup plus 2 tablespoons powdered sugar
* 1 large egg plus 1 large egg yolk, at room temperature
* 1 teaspoon vanilla extract
* 2½ cups all-purpose flour, plus more for dusting
* ½ teaspoon kosher salt
* 1⅓ cups Caramelized Banana & Jackfruit Jam (page 27)

1   Place the butter and ¾ cup of the powdered sugar in the bowl of a stand mixer fitted with the paddle attachment. Cream on medium-high speed until light and fluffy, 3 to 4 minutes.

2   Mix in the egg and egg yolk one at a time. After each addition, make sure to beat until the mixture is well combined and the egg is fully incorporated. Add in the vanilla. Scrape down the bottom and sides of the bowl with a rubber spatula.

3   Adjust the speed of the mixer to low. Gradually stir in the flour and salt until just incorporated. Turn off the mixer and give the dough a couple of folds.

4   Split the dough in half and wrap each dough ball in plastic wrap. Let the dough chill for at least 1 hour in the fridge.

*Continued*

5   Position a rack in the middle of the oven and preheat the oven to 350°F. Line four baking sheets with silicone mats.

6   Lightly flour a rolling pin and your work surface. Take one of the dough balls and plop it on your work surface. Roll dough out until it's 1/8 inch thick. Make sure to pick up the dough and occasionally sprinkle some flour between rolls so it doesn't stick.

7   Using a 2-inch flower-shaped cookie cutter, cut out as many flower shapes as possible from the dough. Place the flowers on the lined baking sheets, spacing them at least 1 inch apart. For half of the flowers, cut out a circle of dough from the center of each one using a 1-inch round cookie cutter. These hollow flowers will act as a the windows of the final sandwich cookies. Gather and reroll the scraps until you have about 60 flower cookies, half of which are the hollow windows.

8   Bake two of the prepared baking sheets for 8 to 10 minutes, or until the edges are golden brown. Transfer the cookies to a wire rack to cool completely. Repeat the baking process with the other two baking sheets containing the remaining flower cookies.

9   Take the other ball of dough out of the fridge. Repeat the rolling, shaping, and cutting process until you have about 60 flower cookies, half of which are the hollow windows.

10   Bake two of the prepared baking sheets for 8 to 10 minutes, or until the edges are golden brown. Transfer the cookies to a wire rack to cool completely. Repeat the baking process with the other two baking sheets containing the remaining cookies.

11   Using a small sieve, dust the tops of the cookie windows with the remaining 2 tablespoons powdered sugar. Line up each cookie window with a corresponding whole cookie to make a matching pair.

12   Flip over the whole flower halves so that they are flat side up. Using an offset spatula, spread about 1 teaspoon of the jam on the surface of each cookie. Top each layer with a cookie window, so that it forms a cookie sandwich with some jam visible in the center. Store any leftovers in an airtight container at room temperature for up to 3 days.

# Melts My Heart

On the eve of my first commencement ceremony, I dragged my roommates Michelle, Yensy, and Lauren out to Fentons Creamery in Oakland to cross the Fentons Challenge off my bucket list. It was something I had been patiently waiting to complete ever since I'd heard about it as a freshman. I even wore my graduation cap for the occasion. For years, I had heard of brave students before me going to this ice cream parlor to devour the banana split in less than fifteen minutes. The reward was a free T-shirt. You still had to pay for the sundae itself, but the glory was priceless.

When I turned twenty-one a year prior, I tried doing the same thing, but the staff wouldn't let me attempt the challenge because I didn't have a specific voucher that came in the *Daily Cal* school newspaper. This time around, I wanted to redeem myself before I had to leave the East Bay behind. I proudly presented the newspaper clipping and took my seat at the table. I had watched YouTube videos from competitive food eaters about techniques on eating ice cream as fast as possible, so I requested a cup of hot water to help me in my efforts.

With iPhones at the ready to film, I was given the dish piled high with three gargantuan scoops of ice cream, chocolate syrup, and mountains of whipped cream. The timer started and I immediately got to shoveling spoonfuls of ice cream into my mouth. I thought I was keeping a good pace, glugging hot water in between the first few bites of vanilla, then strawberry. It helped alleviate the brain freezes at first. Then, slowly but surely, I began to lose steam. My once excited eyes no longer wanted to look at the mass of semiliquid ice cream before me. I was probably only seven minutes into the challenge, but I was ready to throw in the towel. I was consoled by all my supportive friends cheering me on and leisurely enjoying their own normal-size bowls of ice cream.

After the fifteen minutes were up, the

waitress came back and regretfully announced that I was out of time. I was slumped in my seat, and all you could see were melting puddles of ice cream murky like the snow in New York City two days after a blizzard. I rushed over to the bathroom, and I remember immediately throwing up into a toilet bowl. The worst part? The ice cream was still cold when it came up! It was a walk of shame going back to my friends' booth, but they triple-checked if I was okay. I might have been the Fentons Challenge loser that night, but I was happy that I got to have this last hurrah with people I loved. As my roommates and I chatted about our graduation gowns and how excited we were to see our families the next day, I felt like a winner for having such good friends who would support me through thick and thin.

# Ube Skillet Crinkle Cookie

*Makes 1 (7 ½-inch) skillet cookie*

When I brought over my KitchenAid stand mixer from California on a flight from SFO to JFK (in a duffel bag, no less!), I was so relieved it made it through airport security. In my first apartment in Crown Heights, I used it to bake ube crinkle cookies for my roommates and me. I wanted to make a version of the moist, powdered sugar–topped ube crinkle cookies from Kape Republik, a Filipino coffee shop and bakery in Cerritos, California. My family in Southern California shared some with me back in 2016, and I was itching to have a taste of them on the East Coast.

For this recipe, I also wanted to re-create the Pizookie from BJ's, one of my favorite comfort chain restaurants. There are BJ's locations nationwide, and the closest one to me in Stockton was on Pacific Avenue. After tennis practice in high school, my friend and teammate Chelsea would drive us to BJ's just for dessert. Without fail, we would get the signature Pizookie, usually the chocolate chip flavor with vanilla ice cream. My eyes would pop out of my skull every time I saw the giant cookies served in hot cast iron skillets and topped with scoops of melty ice cream. Baked ube crinkle dough makes for an ideal skillet cookie with its chewy center and crisp edges. I also like doubling up on the ube flavor by piling ube ice cream on top of the cookie.

* Nonstick spray
* 4 tablespoons (½ stick) unsalted butter, at room temperature
* ¼ cup granulated sugar
* ¼ cup packed dark brown sugar
* I large egg, at room temperature
* ¼ cup store-bought ube halaya (see Note)
* ½ tablespoon ube extract
* ¾ cup plus 2 tablespoons all-purpose flour
* I teaspoon baking powder
* ½ teaspoon kosher salt
* 2 tablespoons powdered sugar
* Ube ice cream (Magnolia brand preferred), for serving

*Note: The homemade ube halaya recipes on page 24 in the Jams, Syrups & Toppings chapter contain a significant amount of milk in them, which result in the baked cookie having a cakier texture. I prefer the store-bought kind for this recipe in particular to achieve a chewy crinkle cookie.*

1   Position a rack in the middle of the oven and preheat the oven to 325°F. Grease a 7½-inch cast iron skillet with nonstick spray and set aside.

*Continued*

2    Place the butter, granulated sugar, and brown sugar in the bowl of a stand mixer fitted with the paddle attachment. Beat together on medium-high speed until light and fluffy, 1 to 2 minutes. Mix in the egg, ube halaya, and ube extract until the mixture is well combined. Scrape down the sides and bottom of the bowl with a rubber spatula.

3    In a separate small bowl, whisk the flour, baking powder, and salt until the baking powder is evenly distributed. Adjust the mixer to the lowest speed and gradually stir in the flour mixture until it forms a dough and there are little to no flour streaks.

4    Using the rubber spatula, transfer the sticky dough to the greased skillet until it's a smooth layer that reaches the edges of the pan. With a small sieve, dust the entire surface of the cookie with the powdered sugar.

5    Bake for 32 to 35 minutes, or until the cookie has puffed up and set. Cool in the pan for 10 minutes and serve warm with scoops of ube ice cream. It's best eaten straightaway.

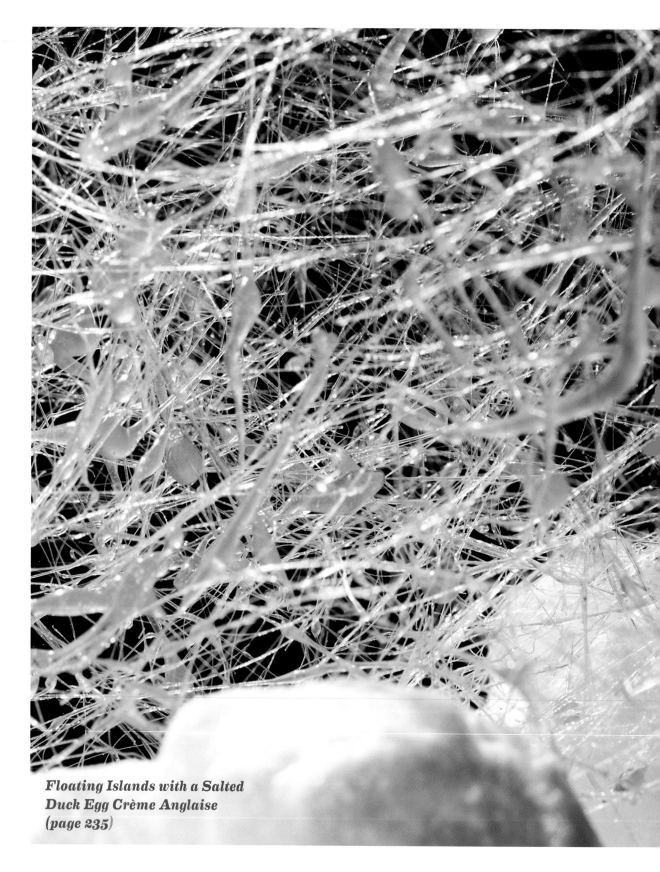

*Floating Islands with a Salted
Duck Egg Crème Anglaise*
(page 235)

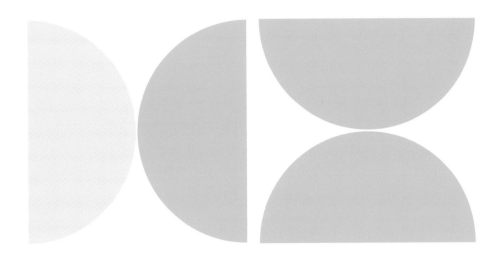

# PART V
## Brooklyn, New York

*New City, New Me*

CW: Violence

**When I first moved to New York, it wasn't some lifelong goal that I had written about in a manifestation journal. I watched rom-com after rom-com set there, but it always seemed too fast-paced for a California girl like me. After graduating from UC Berkeley in May 2017, I didn't have a job lined up, and I was filled with dread at the prospect of having to move back home with my parents in Stockton. Throughout the two months of my postgrad unemployment, I had only imagined myself living in San Francisco, where I could hang out with the majority of my friends, who were starting their "adulting" journey without me. I daydreamed about renting my own cozy apartment in the Mission District and riding the trolley to a high-rise office in SoMa. But every day was a game of LinkedIn roulette, filling out cover letters, and sending them to no avail.**

**O***verall, I took it really hard* having the independence I gained in college stripped away from me. Moving back home felt like I was taking one step forward and two steps back. Don't get me wrong! I was thankful that my parents even allowed me to stay in my childhood bedroom. It was just not what I envisioned for myself. At the time, I likened it to purgatory, an interminable period of arrested development. I wasn't used to living under my parents' roof and rules again, and not having a lot of agency to get around when I didn't drive a car.

When it was my best friend Michelle's birthday, I had to beg my dad to drop me off at the Dublin/Pleasanton BART station so I could go visit her in San Francisco.

During that fateful trip, I scheduled an in-person interview at a marketing agency on my last day there. I thought it went well (even though I never heard back from them), and I was coming off the high of seeing all my friends again when I took a seat on the BART train back home. Little did I know, this train ride would change the course of my life. Two strangers jumped me from behind as the doors opened at my station. They slammed me to the ground, trying to wrench my phone out of my hands. Since I had a death grip on it, they stole my Longchamp purse instead, which had my wallet and everything else I'd brought with me. In my state of shock, I could only start screaming for help, and another guy on the train started running after them. He came back with my bag, but the strangers made off with my money and ID.

I called my mom in tears to come get me, and I don't think I've ever felt as scared or awful as I did at that moment. I replayed the scene in my head over and over again. Why me? What did I do to deserve this? It wasn't that late and I wasn't alone. How come they chose me? My mom was worried out of her mind when I got to the car, and I was despondent. When I got home, all I could do was cry.

It wasn't easy for me to continue staying with my parents after that because I felt like I was even more of a failure. I had gotten mugged less than a year earlier, and this time hurt me even more. Mentally, physically, emotionally . . . I was at my lowest point. I didn't have the energy to talk to my family much or leave my room, let alone get back in the kitchen to bake for fun. I fell into a hard depression, and I went to a therapist who didn't help me feel better. My mom would always tell me, "Do your best and God will do the rest." And it was during this period that I felt like no amount of prayer could enact the change I wanted to see in my life. At some point, my resolve was to try and move as

far away as possible. I started applying to jobs only in New York, and I spruced up my own music blog in hopes of turning it into something more. In between interviewing indie artists on their experiences as BIPOC in the industry, I got an email from a live music company called Bandsintown based in Manhattan asking if I was available for a Skype call. The rest is history.

As soon as I got that job offer and told my parents, my dad was very happy for me. However, my mom couldn't hide her disapproval that I'd be moving so far away. For her, it was as if I were committing a cardinal sin by deserting the family. God forbid you live more than a twenty-minute drive from your closest relatives! Eventually, she stopped clicking her tongue enough to assist me with the moving process. Before I even received the news about working for Bandsintown, my family and I already had a big trip to the East Coast planned. Instead of packing for a short visit, I stuffed my belongings destined for New York into everyone else's carry-on luggage. During that visit, we stayed with my auntie Tess, uncle Tan, and my cousins Anna and JB in Fords, New Jersey.

They drove me to Crown Heights to meet up with Ate Molly's friend Lana. We toured an apartment together, signed a lease with her friend Milly, and got the keys, all in the span of a week. On the day that I signed the lease, Anna and I went to Roberta's in Bushwick to commemorate this huge life event with pizza. We gleefully devoured each slice of the Bee Sting, which was covered in spicy soppressata and hot honey. Everything happened so quickly, and it was so exhilarating. It made me all the more excited to start anew. After coming back to California to tie up loose ends and to bid farewell to my loved ones in August, I took a one-way flight to JFK listening to "Empire State of Mind" on repeat.

My room in that first apartment was about the size of a closet. I could only fit a twin-size bed in there, but I didn't care! (We would later experience every problem under the sun, ranging from inept landlords to cockroaches to broken radiators, but that's a story for a different day.) On average, you'd find twenty-two-year-old me at a show four to five nights a week anyways. I was in a state of nirvana while drinking up New York's boundless energy that summer. Even getting caught in the rain felt like magic. The city was teeming with so much life, and that electricity galvanized me to jump out of my comfort zone. No longer was I a wallflower. I somehow had the courage to strike up conversations with anyone and everyone. I took up the habit of using my lunch breaks to window-shop at Dover Street Market, and the staff working there became some of my first friends.

I loved that I could take the subway for $2.75 and step out onto streets I had never set foot on before. Jaywalking across busy intersections in Midtown felt like that montage in *The Devil Wears Prada* where Anne Hathaway sprints to work in myriad stunning outfits after her makeover. Even when I got accustomed to my daily commute, the frequency of it didn't make it feel any less special. Whenever I hopped on the Q train back to Brooklyn after work and saw the gorgeous skyline at sunset, it made my breath catch in my throat. The majesty of it made me forget that I was wedged between bodies of other rush-hour passengers like sardines in a can. And on my walk from the Eastern Parkway train stop past the Brooklyn Museum, I could catch glimpses into the monstera-lined windows of other shoebox apartments and see that our little lives were all interconnected. Just living in the concrete jungle that is New York makes you feel like you're part of something bigger than yourself.

In the span of a year, I learned so many lessons, including the following:

**I'm not built for snowstorms.**

**I can't subsist on pink Starbursts and takeout alone.**

**No one from here calls it the Big Apple.**

**It's pronounced "Gren-itch" Village and not like the color *green*.**

**Tribeca stands for the "Triangle Below Canal Street."**

**Google the apartment address + "bedbugs" before signing a lease.**

**You can take New York at your own pace. There's a pocket of the city meant for everyone who lives here.**

After those frenzied first few months in New York, I grew tired of excessive stimuli, and the initial euphoria faded into contentment tinged with sadness. As I was making friends and building a life here at breakneck speed, I felt like I was forsaking the people who shaped the person I was. What does it mean when you move more than two thousand miles away from all your anchors? I was a ship unmoored. It was the first time in my life that I didn't have a strong, close-knit Filipino network of people I could turn to. Lack of proximity to other Filipinos made me feel lost. There was always a part of me that missed my family and friends in California, and I still do. It must have been remnants of Catholic guilt that made me feel like I wasn't calling enough and that I was a bad daughter for leaving my parents to take care of Argeli by themselves. I used secrecy as a mode of self-preservation. Instead of telling them when I had bad days because I didn't want to worry them, I'd give them vague anecdotes about work and that was it. I put a lot of pressure on myself to prove to them that uprooting my life to another coast wasn't all for naught. It didn't help that my mom would FaceTime me just to ask when I'd come back home for good.

This *utang na loob* made me feel grateful toward my family for helping me get to this point. But on the other hand, it also made me resentful that I couldn't live up to the expectations that they projected onto me. In part, I retreated into myself when the pressure felt too great to be perfect. There was a lot that I had to unpack on my own, and I'm glad that I had that space to put myself first. Until I found myself on the opposite side of the country, I felt like I couldn't do that work. Distance really does make the heart grow fonder, and it eventually helped me create healthier boundaries between myself and my parents.

When I visited California in September 2018, I spent some time with my favorite people in the Bay Area. My week was jam-packed with hanging out with pals I hadn't seen in months. On one of those nights, Michael, Ate Sydney's boyfriend, picked me up and drove me to the top of Twin Peaks to see the stars. As I vented to him about feeling overwhelmed and not having enough of myself to go around, he reassured me that it was okay to slow down. He listened to me as I regaled him with cheerier stories about what I'd been up to since I moved, and he said that he was proud of me. Before we left the summit, he turned to me and said, "There's a distinct turning point where you can divide your life into before and after. For me, that was meeting Sydney. For you, that must be New York."

He was right. To this day, I think about how those first couple of years here laid the foundation for the person that I am today. People have told me that you've gotta live in New York for at least ten years to be considered a real New Yorker. Although I haven't exactly made it to a decade yet, I've lived here long enough to know that it's irrevocably changed me for the better.

*Jumbo Calamansi Poppy Seed
Muffins with Tangy Glaze
(page 199)*

# BREADS & FRIED TREATS

As much as Filipinos have an affinity for rice in the form of kaka-nin or jasmine rice with every savory meal, we also have a soft spot for all types of breads and fried treats. Whether I'm at my local bagel shop in Bed-Stuy or baking fresh-baked pandesal, Filipino bread rolls, I can't say no to anything hot from an oven or fryer.

# Basic Pandesal

### *Makes 24 rolls*

Pandesal is a Filipino bread roll that you typically eat for breakfast or an afternoon snack. It reminds me of a King's Hawaiian Sweet Roll, but each soft, fluffy roll is dusted with a layer of breadcrumbs. There's nothing more comforting than hot pandesal on a Saturday morning. When I was a kid, my parents would bring home bags from Valerio's City Bakery in Berry-essa. I'd eat a roll toasted with a generous spread of butter and sprinkling of sugar. Other times, I'd dip it in dinuguan, a Filipino pork blood and vinegar stew, or have two slices of pandesal filled with corned beef for lunch. You don't necessarily need a stand mixer or heavy machinery to make pandesal because you can knead the dough with your hands.

* 1 cup whole milk
* $2\frac{1}{4}$ teaspoons active dry yeast
* $\frac{1}{2}$ cup sugar
* $2\frac{1}{4}$ cups all-purpose flour
* 2 cups bread flour
* $1\frac{3}{4}$ teaspoons kosher salt
* 2 large eggs, at room temperature
* 4 tablespoons ($\frac{1}{2}$ stick) unsalted butter, at room temperature, cut into tablespoon-size pieces
* Nonstick spray
* 2 tablespoons plain breadcrumbs

1  In a small microwave-safe measuring cup, heat the milk in the microwave for 30-second intervals until it reaches 108°F to 110°F. Stir in active dry yeast and 2 teaspoons of the sugar. Let sit 10 minutes for the yeast to bubble up. It will look foamy once activated.

2  In a large bowl, whisk 2 cups of the all-purpose flour, the bread flour, and salt. Lightly flour your work surface with the remaining $\frac{1}{4}$ cup all-purpose flour.

3  Using a wooden spoon, mix the yeast mixture, eggs, remaining sugar, and butter into the large bowl with the flour mixture. Once it forms a shaggy dough, turn the contents over onto your lightly floured surface.

4  Knead until the dough passes the windowpane test and forms a smooth ball, 10 to 12 minutes. To perform the windowpane test, grab

*Continued*

a piece of dough and carefully stretch it apart with your fingers into a square shape. If the dough is translucent in the center and doesn't tear, you're done kneading.

5    Grease another large bowl with nonstick spray. Place the kneaded dough ball in it and cover with plastic wrap. Let it proof at room temperature for about 1 hour, or until it doubles in size.

6    Place the breadcrumbs in a small bowl and set aside.

7    Set the plastic wrap aside and punch the risen dough down. Divide into 24 equal portions. I like to do this by weight with a kitchen scale.

8    Line a baking sheet with a silicone mat. Grab one of the portions of dough. Cover the remaining dough portions with the plastic wrap while you work on shaping one at a time. Flatten the dough portion into a circle with your palm. Pick up the edges of the flattened dough, pleat them, and pinch the dough at the top to seal.

9    Place the dough ball seam side down. Roll into a smoother ball with your hand enclosed over it like a claw moving in a circular motion. Once nice and round, roll the ball all over in the breadcrumbs. Place the dough balls 1 inch apart on the lined baking sheet. Repeat the process until all the dough portions are shaped, rolled, and coated in crumbs.

10    Cover the surface of the dough balls with a kitchen towel, so that they don't dry out. Let them rise for 55 to 60 minutes, until they double in size. At the 30-minute mark, position a rack in the middle of the oven and preheat the oven to 350°F.

11    Once the dough balls have doubled in size, remove the kitchen towel, and transfer the baking sheet to the oven. Bake for 15 to 20 minutes, or until the pandesal are golden brown. Transfer the baking sheet to a wire rack to let the pandesal cool slightly before serving. The pandesal are best served warm, but you can store any leftovers in an airtight container at room temperature for up to 3 days.

# Ube Melon Pandesal

*Makes 12 rolls*

Back in October 2018, I visited Japan with my parents and my little sister, Argeli. Traveling and checking out all the tourist spots together was a magical experience. I was also thrilled that we were able to try so much incredible food. Three years later, the memory of buying a warm melon pan in Tokyo flooded back to me when I was planning the menu for a local pop-up at Land to Sea, a coffee shop in East Williamsburg. I knew I wanted to use ube for a sweet bread, so a hybrid melon pan and pandesal was the ideal vehicle for it. Similar to Mexican conchas, melon pan is a type of Japanese sweet bread that has a crunchy cookie topping designed to resemble a melon.

For my version, I flavored my basic pandesal dough with ube extract and filled it with ube halaya for an extra-creamy texture inside. Then, I topped the rolls with an ube cookie topping dusted with breadcrumbs and sugar. Coming up with the recipe title's portmanteau was so much fun that it helped my creative juices flow in finding the aforementioned ways to bring the fusion flavors and elements together. The ube melon pandesal sold out at Land to Sea in less than an hour, and now I'm excited to share the recipe with you.

* 10 tablespoons (1 stick plus 2 tablespoons) unsalted butter, at room temperature
* 1 cup powdered sugar
* 3 large eggs, at room temperature
* 2 tablespoons ube extract
* 1³/₈ teaspoons kosher salt
* 1 teaspoon baking powder
* 3¹/₄ cups cake flour
* ¹/₂ cup whole milk
* 1¹/₈ teaspoons active dry yeast
* ¹/₄ cup plus 2 tablespoons granulated sugar
* 1 cup plus 2 tablespoons all-purpose flour
* 1 cup bread flour
* Nonstick spray
* 2 tablespoons plain breadcrumbs
* ³/₄ cup ube halaya, store-bought or homemade (page 24)

1    Place 1 stick of the unsalted butter and the powdered sugar in the bowl of a stand mixer fitted with the paddle attachment. Cream on medium-high speed until light and fluffy, 3 to 4 minutes. Mix in two eggs, one at a time, and add in 1 tablespoon of the ube extract. Scrape down the bottom and sides of the bowl with a rubber spatula.

2    Whisk together ¹/₂ teaspoon of the salt, the baking powder, and cake flour in a medium bowl until well combined. Adjust the speed of the mixer to low. Gradually stir in the flour mixture until a cookie dough forms. Wrap the dough in plastic wrap. Transfer the dough to the fridge and chill for at least 2 hours.

*Continued*

**3** In a small microwave-safe measuring cup, heat the milk in the microwave for 30-second intervals until it reaches 108°F to 110°F. Stir in the yeast and 1 teaspoon of the granulated sugar. Let sit for 10 minutes to allow the yeast to bubble up. It will look foamy once activated.

**4** In a large bowl, whisk 1 cup of the all-purpose flour, the bread flour, and $^7/_8$ teaspoon of the salt. Lightly flour your work surface with the remaining 2 tablespoons all-purpose flour.

**5** Using a wooden spoon, mix the yeast mixture, remaining 1 egg, $^1/_4$ cup (minus 1 teaspoon) of the granulated sugar, and the remaining 2 tablespoons butter into the large bowl with the flour mixture. Once it forms a shaggy dough, turn the contents over onto your lightly floured surface.

**6** Knead the remaining 1 tablespoon ube extract into the dough until it becomes a smooth ball, has a homogenous purple color, and passes the windowpane test, 10 to 12 minutes. If you want to avoid temporarily staining your hands, you can wear gloves.

**7** Grease another large bowl with nonstick spray. Place the kneaded dough ball in it and cover with plastic wrap. Let it proof at room temperature for about 1 hour, or until it doubles in size.

**8** Line a baking sheet with a silicone mat and set aside. Mix the breadcrumbs with the remaining 2 tablespoons granulated sugar in a small bowl and set aside. Take the chilled ube cookie dough out of the fridge and divide into 12 equal portions, rolling them into balls. Set aside.

9   Once the pandesal dough has risen, set the plastic wrap aside and punch down the risen dough. Divide into 12 equal portions. I like to do this by weight with a kitchen scale. Grab one of the portions of pandesal dough. Cover the remaining dough portions with the plastic wrap while you work on shaping one at a time. Flatten the dough portion into a 5-inch circle with a rolling pin.

10   Place 1 tablespoon of the ube halaya in the center. Pick up the edges of the flattened dough, pleat them over the halaya, and pinch the dough at the top to seal.

11   Place the dough ball seam side down. Roll into a smoother ball with your hand enclosed over it like a claw moving in a circular motion. Once nice and round, set aside. Using your palm, flatten one of the ube cookie dough balls into a 3-inch circle. Cover the top of the shaped ube pandesal ball with the cookie dough circle.

12   Using a bench scraper or knife, gently score the cookie dough topping into a crisscross pattern. Dip the top of the pandesal in the breadcrumb mixture. Place each melon pandesal ball 1 inch apart on the prepared baking sheet. Repeat the process until all the dough portions are shaped, coated in crumbs, and scored.

13   Cover the surface of the dough balls with a kitchen towel, so that they don't dry out. Let them rise for 55 to 60 minutes, until they double in size. At the 30-minute mark, position a rack in the middle of the oven and preheat the oven to 350°F.

14   Once the dough balls have doubled in size, remove the kitchen towel, and transfer the baking sheet to the oven. Bake for 15 to 20 minutes, or until the melon pandesal are golden brown. Transfer the baking sheet to a wire rack to let the melon pandesal cool slightly before serving. The melon pandesal are best served warm, but you can store any leftovers in an airtight container at room temperature for up to 2 days.

# Peach Mango Cheesecake Turon

*Makes 16 turon*

Sweet and crispy turon usually contains saba bananas, which make up the bulk of the filling. Saba bananas are starchier than Cavendish bananas, which are the most common variety sold at grocery stores in the United States. Since saba bananas are often cooked before they are eaten, they are similar to plantains. Inspired by Jollibee's trademark fried peach mango pies, I wanted to experiment with an entirely different turon filling by incorporating a compote of those fruits instead of just banana and jackfruit.

Using store-bought spring roll wrappers quickens the process of assembling the rolls. I also added a cheesecake filling flavored with lemon zest for a bright contrast to the peach mango compote. Similar to classic turon, they get a final coating of caramel. You can keep the assembled turon in the freezer to fry whenever you have a hankering for peach mango pies. The only change to keep in mind is that the initial frying time will increase 3 to 4 minutes per side. The peach mango cheesecake turon taste just as good as, if not better than, Jollibee's celebrated dessert menu item.

* 2 (8-ounce) blocks cream cheese, left to soften at room temperature for 1 hour
* ½ cup powdered sugar, sifted
* 1 tablespoon fresh lemon juice
* Zest of 1 lemon
* ¼ teaspoon kosher salt
* 16 (8-inch square) frozen individual spring roll wrappers
* 1 cup Peach Mango Compote (page 29), cold
* Vegetable oil, for frying
* ½ cup packed dark brown sugar, for caramel coating

1   Place the blocks of softened cream cheese in a medium bowl. Stir in the powdered sugar, lemon juice, lemon zest, and salt with a wooden spoon until the filling is smooth and there are no lumps. Cover the bowl with plastic wrap and place in the fridge until you're ready to assemble the turon.

2   Remove the spring roll wrappers from the freezer and place on a plate to thaw. Take a paper towel moistened with some water to cover the wrappers to prevent them from drying out.

3   Place the compote in a small bowl. Position the compote and another small bowl containing ¼ cup water near you so you're ready for rolling the turon. Transfer the cream cheese filling to a piping bag fitted with a large round tip.

*Continued*

4    Take one wrapper and set it in front of you on a flat work surface so that it's a diamond shape. Pipe about 2 tablespoons of the cream cheese filling in the middle of the wrapper. It should form a 5-inch log straight across. Scoop about 1 tablespoon of the peach mango compote on top. Dip your finger with water and lightly dampen the edges of the wrapper.

5    Fold the bottom corner over the log, and then fold both the left and right sides toward the center. Roll the wrapper up toward the top corner, using more water to seal if necessary. Repeat with the rest of the turon.

6    Fill a 10¼-inch cast iron skillet with enough vegetable oil to come ¾ inch up the sides. Heat the oil over medium-high heat until it reaches 350°F. Have a wire rack set over a baking sheet nearby.

7    Fry three or four turon at a time, just enough not to overcrowd the pan. Fry until golden brown, 1 to 2 minutes on each side. Using metal tongs, transfer the cooked turon to the wire rack set over a baking sheet. Repeat the frying process with the rest of the turon.

8    Once all the turon are fried, sprinkle the brown sugar directly into the oil. Quickly dunk as many turon as can fit in the pan and toss around in the melted sugar for 10 seconds. Return the caramelized turon to the wire rack and repeat the process with the remaining turon. Keep in mind that the sugar will start to burn after 1 minute of being in the oil. Let the turon cool for about 5 minutes so the filling doesn't burn your tongue. The turon are best served warm and should all be eaten the same day that they are fried.

# Jumbo Calamansi Poppy Seed Muffins with a Tangy Glaze

*Makes 6 jumbo muffins*

I've spoken about Costco at least once in this book, and I'll do it again! As much as I used to think that Sundays in my family revolved around going to mass, let's be real. My parents schlepped us to a series of grocery stores after church, and Costco, which was the highlight of my day, was the biggest of them all. When I wheeled our cart to the bakery section, I never hesitated to grab the variety pack of double chocolate chip, blueberry, and almond poppy jumbo muffins. After bringing them home, I'd cut them up into quarters so we'd have enough to share. I think these giant calamansi poppy seed muffins, a play on lemon poppy but with a Philippine lime, would make a charming addition to the Costco lineup.

The Yakult glaze adds another element of tang to the citrus in the muffins. Bottles of this Japanese probiotic drink were always around in my youth. I used to think that they were the better version of Danimals yogurt smoothies. Since the film adaptation of *To All the Boys I've Loved Before* referenced it, I swear Yakult has become even more ubiquitous in recent years. Either way, I think the more Yakult there is in the world, the merrier.

## Muffins

* 3 cups all-purpose flour
* 1³/₄ cups granulated sugar
* 1 tablespoon baking powder
* ¹/₂ teaspoon baking soda
* ¹/₂ teaspoon kosher salt
* 2 tablespoons poppy seeds
* 2 large eggs, at room temperature, lightly whisked
* 1³/₄ cups buttermilk, at room temperature
* ¹/₄ cup vegetable oil
* 8 tablespoons (1 stick) unsalted butter, melted
* 1 teaspoon vanilla extract
* Zest of 1 lime
* 6 ounces frozen calamansi juice, thawed

## Glaze

* ³/₄ cup powdered sugar, sifted
* 1¹/₂ tablespoons Yakult

## Muffins

1   Position a rack in the middle of the oven and preheat the oven to 425°F. While leaving alternating spaces open, line two 6-cup jumbo muffin tins with liners. There should be 3 lined

*Continued*

muffin cavities per tin. You want those empty spaces since the muffin tops spread and rise a lot!

2   Whisk together the flour, I cup of the granulated sugar, the baking powder, baking soda, salt, and poppy seeds in a large bowl.

3   Create a large well in the center of the bowl, and then add in the eggs, buttermilk, vegetable oil, melted butter, vanilla, and lime zest. Stirring from the center of the well, whisk the ingredients by hand until the batter is smooth and no flour streaks remain.

4   Fill each lined jumbo muffin cavity up to the top with batter, a little under I cup per cavity.

5   Bake for 7 minutes and then turn down the heat to 350°F. Bake for an additional I7 to 20 minutes, or until a toothpick inserted into the center of one muffin comes out clean.

6   While the muffins are baking, make a calamansi syrup by combining the thawed calamansi juice with the remaining ³/₄ cup granulated sugar in a small saucepan. Cook over medium-low heat, stirring occasionally with a rubber spatula, until it reaches a boil. Continue to cook for an additional 3 to 5 minutes, or until the sugar has dissolved and the liquid reduces a bit. Turn off the heat.

7   When you take the muffins out of the oven, immediately poke six to eight toothpick holes in the top of each. Using a pastry brush, generously brush the tops with the syrup. Let the muffins cool in the tins for at least I0 minutes to soak up the liquid. Remove the muffins from the tins and transfer to a wire cooling rack.

### Glaze

8   In a small bowl, whisk together the powdered sugar and Yakult until smooth. Drizzle the tops of the muffins with the glaze and let it harden for at least I0 minutes before serving. Store any leftovers in an airtight container in the fridge for up to 4 days.

# Food for the Gods Banana Bread

*Makes one 9 × 5-inch loaf*

When I was younger, my family used to lovingly call my cousin "Anna Banana" for years. I consider Anna my best friend, even now that we're adults. It wasn't until I moved to New York that I got a chance to live on the same coast as her. When I'd call her in between her nursing shifts to keep in touch, she'd tell me about how she occasionally spent her time off making banana bread for my auntie Tess and uncle Tan. This banana bread recipe is inspired by Anna and Food for the Gods, a Filipino walnut and date bar usually served at Christmastime.

* Nonstick spray
* ½ cup raw walnuts
* ¾ cup pitted dates
* ½ teaspoon kosher salt
* 1 teaspoon baking soda
* 2 cups all-purpose flour
* 8 tablespoons (1 stick) unsalted butter, at room temperature
* ⅔ cup packed dark brown sugar
* 2 large eggs, at room temperature
* 1 teaspoon vanilla extract
* 2 cups mashed ripe banana (about 4 medium bananas)
* ⅓ cup sour cream, at room temperature

1   Position a rack in the middle of the oven and preheat the oven to 350°F. Grease a 9 × 5-inch loaf pan with nonstick spray and line with parchment paper. You want enough overhang on two sides to be able to lift the baked banana bread out with ease later.

2   Place the walnuts in a small saucepan set over medium-high heat. Stir frequently with a wooden spoon and toast until lightly browned and fragrant, 4 to 6 minutes. Turn off the heat. Transfer the walnuts to a cutting board, chop them finely, and place them in a medium bowl. On the same cutting board, chop each pitted date into six pieces. Transfer the chopped dates to the bowl.

3   Whisk in the salt, baking soda, and flour. Make sure the dates and walnuts are all evenly distributed in the dry mixture. Set aside.

4   Place the butter and brown sugar in the bowl of a stand mixer fitted with the paddle attachment. Cream together on medium-high speed until light and fluffy, 3 to 4 minutes. Add the

eggs, one at a time, and then beat in the vanilla. Scrape down the bowl with a rubber spatula and mix in the mashed banana and sour cream until just incorporated.

5    Adjust the mixer to the lowest speed and gradually add in the flour mixture. Stir for 1 to 2 minutes, then scrape down the sides and bottom of the bowl. Stir again until no flour pockets remain.

6    Pour the batter into the lined loaf pan. Bake for 60 to 65 minutes, or until a toothpick inserted into the center of the bread comes out clean. Let the bread cool in the pan for 15 minutes before lifting out and letting it cool completely on a wire rack. Slice before serving. Store any leftovers in an airtight container at room temperature for up to 4 days.

# Christmas Star Bread with Pan de Regla Filling

*Makes 16 servings*

Pan de regla sold in Philippine bakeries is a bread roll with a bright-red vanilla custard filling that gets to this shade of crimson with the help of food coloring. *Regla* is the Tagalog word for "menstruation," which gives meaning to its bloodlike color. The bread is also called kalihim, or "secret," because it was once a big secret that the custard is made with bread baked from the day before.

Since I like to make Christmas star bread to get into the holiday spirit, I wanted to include this sweet filling in my recipe. Instead of just having the pan de regla filling for one individual roll, I thought it would be more fun for the family to pull the bread apart with the custard woven throughout it. Not to mention, the finished bread has a soft, pillowy texture and looks just like a Christmas parol. Parols are Filipino star-shaped paper lanterns that are colorful and a beautiful addition to any household's Christmas décor. Each bite of the Christmas star bread is so scrumptious that you might just be making this bread all year round. The custard recipe makes more than you'll need for just one star bread, so you can save some for your next batch, or it can be eaten plain and is great on top of a slice of bread.

## Custard Filling

* 2 cups small torn pieces of Basic Pandesal (page 190) or white bread
* 1 cup whole milk, at room temperature
* 1 large egg, at room temperature
* 1/3 cup granulated sugar
* 1/4 teaspoon kosher salt
* 8 to 10 drops red gel food coloring
* 2 tablespoons unsalted butter, at room temperature
* 1 teaspoon vanilla extract

## Bread Dough

* 1 cup whole milk
* 2 1/4 teaspoons active dry yeast
* 1/4 cup granulated sugar
* 4 tablespoons (1/2 stick) unsalted butter, at room temperature, cut into tablespoon-size pieces
* 1 large egg, at room temperature
* 1 teaspoon kosher salt
* 3 1/4 cups all-purpose flour
* Nonstick spray

*Continued*

## Assembly

* 2 large egg yolks, at room temperature
* I tablespoon whole milk, at room temperature
* 2 tablespoons unsalted butter, melted
* I tablespoon powdered sugar

## Custard Filling

1   Place the pandesal pieces in a medium bowl.

2   In a large measuring cup, whisk together the milk, egg, granulated sugar, salt, and red food coloring. Pour the mixture over the pandesal pieces and stir lightly with your whisk. Let sit at room temperature for 8 to I0 minutes for the bread to absorb the milk mixture.

3   Pour the contents of the bowl into a medium saucepan. Cook over medium-low heat, stirring frequently with a wooden spoon, until it forms a thick paste, 5 to 7 minutes. Most of the liquid should be cooked out of the mixture. Immediately stir in the butter and vanilla and mix until smooth. Set aside to cool completely. You can save the custard in an airtight container for up to 4 days in the fridge.

## Bread Dough

4   In a small microwave-safe measuring cup, heat the milk in the microwave for 30-second intervals until it reaches I08°F to II0°F. Stir in the yeast and 2 teaspoons of the granulated sugar. Let sit for I0 minutes for the yeast to bubble up. It will look foamy once activated.

5   Add the yeast mixture to a large bowl. Using a wooden spoon, mix the remaining sugar, the butter, egg, and salt into the bowl until well combined.

6   Stir 3 cups of the flour into the mixture until it forms a shaggy dough. Lightly flour your work surface with the remaining $1/4$ cup flour. Turn the contents of the bowl over onto your lightly floured surface.

7   Knead until it becomes a smooth and elastic dough ball, I5 to I8 minutes. When you poke the dough with your finger, it should spring back. It will be really sticky at first, but keep on kneading until you get there!

8   Grease another large bowl with nonstick spray. Place the kneaded dough ball in it and cover with plastic wrap. Let it proof at room temperature until it doubles in size, about I hour. Line a baking sheet with a silicone mat and set aside.

9   Set the plastic wrap aside and punch the risen dough down. Divide into four equal portions and roll them into balls. Grab one of the dough balls. Cover the remaining balls with the plastic wrap while you work on rolling one at a time. Using a rolling pin, roll out the dough ball into a I0-inch circle. Wrap the dough circle around the rolling pin. Carry it over to the center of the lined baking sheet. Slather $1/3$ cup of the filling over the circle in an even layer on top of the dough.

10   Repeat the process with the rest of the dough portions, stacking each layer of dough and alternating it with the filling, until there is a final layer of rolled-out dough on top. You can stretch the edges of each circle if they aren't perfectly lining up, and you can trim uneven edges with a pizza slicer for a rounder shape.

11   Lightly indent the center of the dough with a $2^{1}/_{2}$-inch round cookie cutter. Starting from

the outer edge of the dough and stopping when you reach the scored circle at the center, make sixteen equal cuts, like the petals of a flower, using a pizza slicer. Grab two adjacent pieces. Twist and rotate the two pieces outward twice, then pinch the edges together with your fingers to form the points of the star. Repeat this process with the rest of the pieces.

## Assembly

12   Cover the shaped star with plastic wrap and let it rise for 25 to 30 minutes, or until it puffs up. While the dough is rising, position a rack in the middle of the oven and preheat the oven to 350°F.

13   Once the dough is risen, remove the plastic wrap. Reseal the edges if the points of the star opened up.

14   In a small bowl, whisk the egg yolks and milk together until smooth. Using a pastry brush, coat the surface of the bread with the egg wash.

15   Bake for 18 to 22 minutes, or until golden brown. Transfer the baking sheet to a wire cooling rack. Using a pastry brush, brush the star bread with the melted butter and let it cool for 7 to 10 minutes. Using a small sieve, top the bread with a light dusting of the powdered sugar before serving warm. Store any leftovers in an airtight container at room temperature for up to 3 days.

# Three-Cheese Ensaymada with Whipped Ricotta, Queso de Bola & Cotija Cheese

*Makes 12 rolls*

Ensaymada are sweet brioche that are products of Spanish colonization in the Philippines. While these spiraled breads first originated in Mallorca, the Filipino variety is commonly topped with butter, sugar, and grated cheese. My version uses a sweetened whipped ricotta that draws some parallels to the acclaimed ricotta toast served at Misi in Williamsburg. I added cotija and queso de bola (also called Edam cheese) for additional sources of salt on top of the whipped ricotta. If you don't have brioche tins, you can use the less expensive, free-standing floret baking cups.

## Bread Dough

* I cup whole milk
* 2¼ teaspoons active dry yeast
* ¼ cup granulated sugar
* 4 tablespoons (½ stick) unsalted butter, at room temperature, cut into tablespoon-size pieces
* I large egg, at room temperature
* I teaspoon kosher salt
* 3¼ cups all-purpose flour
* Nonstick spray

## Assembly

* 2 tablespoons unsalted butter, melted
* ½ cup whole milk ricotta, cold
* ½ cup heavy cream, cold
* ¾ cup powdered sugar, sifted
* ¼ cup grated queso de bola
* 2 tablespoons cotija cheese

## Bread Dough

1   In a small microwave-safe measuring cup, heat the milk in the microwave for 30-second intervals until it reaches 108°F to 110°F. Stir in the yeast and 2 teaspoons of the granulated sugar. Let sit for 10 minutes for the yeast to bubble up. It will look foamy once activated.

2   Add the yeast mixture to a large bowl. Using a wooden spoon, mix in the remaining sugar, the butter, egg, and salt until well combined. Stir 3 cups of the flour into the mixture until it forms a shaggy dough. Lightly flour your work surface with the remaining ¼ cup flour. Turn the contents of the bowl over onto your lightly floured surface.

3   Knead until it becomes a smooth and elastic dough ball, 15 to 18 minutes. When you poke the

*Continued*

dough with your finger, it should spring back. It will be really sticky at first, but keep on kneading until you get there!

4   Grease another large bowl with nonstick spray. Place the kneaded dough ball in it and cover with plastic wrap. Let it proof at room temperature until it doubles in size, about 1 hour.

5   Set the plastic wrap aside and punch the risen dough down. Divide into twelve equal portions and roll them into balls. Line up twelve brioche tins on a baking sheet. Set aside.

6   Grab one of the dough balls. Cover the remaining balls with the plastic wrap while you work on rolling one at a time. Roll the ball into a log that is about 12 inches long. Starting at one end, roll the dough into a coil and tuck the other end underneath it. Rest it gently in one of the baking cups. Repeat the process with the rest of the dough portions until all of them are shaped into spirals.

## Assembly

7   Cover the shaped spirals with plastic wrap and let them rise until they puff up, 25 to 30 minutes.

8   While the dough spirals are rising, position a rack in the middle of the oven and preheat the oven to 350°F.

9   Once the dough spirals are risen, remove the plastic wrap.

10   Bake for 15 to 18 minutes, or until golden brown. Transfer the baking sheet to a wire cooling rack. Using a pastry brush, brush the tops of the ensaymada with the melted butter and let them cool completely before making the whipped ricotta topping.

11   Place the ricotta, heavy cream, and powdered sugar in the bowl of a stand mixer fitted with the whisk attachment.

12   Beat on low speed until the ingredients are incorporated, then increase the speed to medium high. Whip until the mixture is fluffy and forms stiff peaks, 2 to 3 minutes.

13   Transfer the whipped ricotta to a piping bag fitted with a large round tip. Pipe spirals of the ricotta on top of each ensaymada. Sprinkle the grated queso de bola and cotija cheese on top before serving. Store any leftovers in an airtight container in the fridge for up to 3 days.

# Daifuku Carioca

*Makes 9 skewers*

Ichigo daifuku is a Japanese dessert that consists of mochi stuffed with a fresh strawberry nestled in a layer of red bean paste. When my cousin Anna visited me in Crown Heights in May 2021, I treated her to omakase at a Japanese sushi spot called Uotora. After all the high-quality raw fish we had for dinner, the ichigo daifuku we ordered for dessert was a divine addition to the meal. For a Filipino mash-up dessert, I incorporated the flavors of ichigo daifuku into carioca skewers.

Carioca are fried glutinous rice balls coated in a brown sugar glaze that are usually served on bamboo sticks. You can get these sweet, chewy snacks from street vendors in the Philippines. I've taken liberties to add a strawberry glaze and a red bean filling to my recipe. The fried elements and red bean filling are also reminiscent of buchi, another Filipino fried glutinous rice ball that is filled with red bean and covered in sesame seeds.

* 1½ cups plus 3 tablespoons glutinous rice flour
* 1 cup unsweetened, full-fat coconut milk, plus more if needed
* ⅔ cup sweetened red bean mash
* Vegetable oil, for frying
* 1.5 ounces freeze-dried strawberries
* 3 cups powdered sugar, sifted

1  In a medium bowl, mix together the glutinous rice flour and coconut milk by hand until the mixture forms a pliable dough. If your dough still feels too dry, you can add more coconut milk, 1 teaspoon at a time, until it comes together.

2  Portion out 1 tablespoon-sized balls and flatten each as thin as possible. No need for a rolling pin. You can pat each down into a circle with your palm.

3  Place 1 teaspoon of the red bean mash in the middle of the flattened dough circle. Pick up the edges of the dough circle and pleat them so that they enclose the filling. Pinch the dough at the top to seal.

4  Place the dough ball seam side down. Roll into a smoother ball with your hand enclosed over

*Continued*

it like a claw moving in a circular motion. Once nice and round, pierce a chopstick all the way through the carioca ball. This step is key to making sure your dough balls don't explode in the fryer. Without this hole, too much heat builds up inside the carioca and the steam has nowhere to escape.

5   Place the finished carioca balls on a plate. Repeat this filling, rolling, and piercing process with the other dough balls until you have at least 27 carioca in total.

6   Fill a 10¼-inch cast iron skillet with enough vegetable oil to come ¾ inch up the sides. Heat the oil over medium-high heat until it reaches 350°F. Set a wire rack over a baking sheet and have it ready nearby.

7   Cook the dough balls in the oil in batches of four or five at a time so as not to crowd the pan, until they turn golden brown on all sides, 5 to 6 minutes. Using metal tongs, transfer the cooked carioca to the wire cooling rack. Repeat the process until all the carioca are fried.

8   As the carioca are cooling, make the strawberry glaze. In the bowl of a food processor, blitz the freeze-dried strawberries until they turn into a powder. Transfer to a medium bowl.

9   In the medium bowl, whisk the strawberry powder, powdered sugar, and ¾ cup water together until the mixture turns into a smooth glaze.

10   Skewer 3 carioca onto a wooden skewer. Repeat this process with the rest of the carioca until you have 9 skewers total. Coat each carioca skewer in the glaze and transfer to a wire rack for the glaze to harden. The carioca are best served warm and should all be eaten the same day that they are fried.

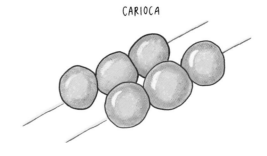

CARIOCA

ICHIGO DAIFUKU

BUCHI
(SESAME BALLS)

# Coconut Palm Sugar Plantain Chips

*Makes 1½ cups*

As an unspoken rule among Filipinos, you must have chichirya, or junk food and snacks, on hand when casually hanging out with friends and family. Chichirya is meant to be shared, and is conducive to good chismis, or gossip. When you're sitting around and chatting up a storm, I personally like to munch on Sun Tropics Saba Banana Chips. They're slightly sweet and crunchy, and I can finish a whole bag by myself. In case I run out of them and, God forbid, they cease to be sold at my local store, I created this recipe as a backup plan. Ripe yellow plantains are a great alternative when you can't find saba bananas. These small-batch chips are fried and flavored with a few pinches of salt and coconut sugar. It should hold you over until your next Pinoy grocery run.

* ¾ teaspoon kosher salt
* 1 large ripe yellow plantain
* Vegetable oil, for frying
* 1 tablespoon coconut palm sugar

1   In a medium bowl, stir together 1 cup water and ½ teaspoon of the salt. Set aside.

2   Peel the plantain and cut it into thin slices. I like to use a vegetable peeler or mandoline for consistently thin slices. Immediately place the cut slices in the saltwater solution.

3   Soak in the solution for 15 minutes. Line a baking sheet with paper towels.

4   After the 15 minutes are up, drain the slices using a large sieve and place them on the lined baking sheet. Pat the tops of the slices dry with another paper towel.

5   Fill a 10¼-inch cast iron skillet with enough vegetable oil to come ¾ inch up the sides. Heat the oil over medium-high heat until it reaches 350°F. Set a wire rack over a baking sheet and have it ready nearby.

6   Add the plantain slices to the oil and cook until golden brown on all sides, 3 to 4 minutes.

7   Using a wire mesh skimmer, transfer the chips to the wire cooling rack and immediately dust with the coconut palm sugar and the remaining ¼ teaspoon kosher salt. The chips taste best warm and served fresh from the fryer.

# Sweet Ukoy (Carrot Fritters)

*Makes 12 ukoy*

Whenever anyone fries ukoy, you'll know it by the tantalizing smell wafting through the house. These Filipino crispy vegetable fritters, usually mixed with whole shrimp, taste delicious with your choice of sawsawan, or vinegar dipping sauce. It's common to eat them as midafternoon snacks or as dinner appetizers. My sweet ukoy is made of grated carrot, and it takes on the spices of a classic carrot cake. It even has a tart sauce that uses pineapple juice instead of vinegar.

* 2 cups grated carrots
  (from about 6 medium carrots)

* ¹/₂ teaspoon kosher salt

* ¹/₂ cup cornstarch

* ¹/₄ cup packed dark brown sugar

* 2 teaspoons ground cinnamon

* ¹/₄ teaspoon ground cloves

* I teaspoon ground nutmeg

* Vegetable oil,
  for frying

* ¹/₄ cup pineapple juice

* 2 cups powdered sugar,
  sifted

* Zest of I lime

SWEET UKOY

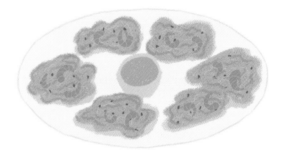

CARROT CAKE

*Continued*

1   Place the grated carrots in a colander set over a medium bowl and sprinkle with the kosher salt. Toss and let the carrots sit for at least 15 minutes.

2   After the 15 minutes are up, squeeze the carrots and strain out as much liquid as possible from them using a cloth. Wring out the cloth three times to dry the carrots, and discard the water.

3   In the medium bowl, mix together the carrots, cornstarch, brown sugar, ground cinnamon, ground cloves, and ground nutmeg with a rubber spatula.

4   Fill a large saucepan with enough oil to coat the bottom and heat the oil over medium-high heat. Once the oil reaches 350°F, drop in 2 tablespoons of batter for each fritter. You can fry up to three or four at a time; just make sure not to overcrowd the pan. Set a wire rack over a baking sheet and have it ready nearby.

5   For each fritter, use a slotted spatula to spread the batter out to create 3-inch circular shapes. Fry until golden brown on both sides, 2 to 3 minutes per side.

6   Transfer the ukoy to the wire cooling rack using the slotted spatula and repeat the process until all your batter is used up.

7   In a small bowl, whisk the pineapple juice, powdered sugar, and lime zest until smooth. Use as a dipping sauce or drizzle on each individual ukoy while they're still warm. The ukoy should all be eaten the same day that they are fried.

# CUSTARDS, PUDDINGS & CHILLED DESSERTS

To beat the heat of a hot and sticky New York summer, these sweet and cold desserts have the power to cool you off better than any A/C unit fit precariously in your window.

# BUKO PANDAN

SHREDDED BUKO

SAGO

NATA DE COCO

GULAMAN CUBES

CONDENSED MILK

PANDAN

KAONG

# CATHEDRAL WINDOW JELLY

# Buko Pandan Cathedral Window Jelly

*Makes 10 servings*

Eating buko pandan salad, a Filipino chilled dessert, is a refreshing and fun textural experience. Each spoonful brings up a mixture of the three following sweet ingredients: kaong, nata de coco, and gulaman. Kaong is the chewy jelly bean–shaped fruit of the palm nut tree. Nata de coco are cubes of coconut gel that are made from fermenting coconut water. Gulaman—the Filipino catch-all word for agar-agar and gelatin-like desserts made using it—is the vegan version of Jell-O that gets flavored with young coconut juice. You can easily find these ingredients at your local Filipino grocery store. The kaong, nata de coco, and gulaman are also submerged in a condensed milk and cream sauce tinted green with pandan extract.

Another Filipino dessert served cold is cathedral window jelly, which is a Christmastime showstopper that has colorful gelatin cubes suspended in a milky gelatin base. Instead of using boxes of rainbow fruit-flavored Jell-O, I thought it would be a novel idea to swap in the main components of buko pandan salad for a monochromatic green look. By merging these desserts into one, you can enjoy the bounciness of the milky gelatin base of cathedral window jelly with the flavors of buko and pandan. The final dessert is also served with a creamy pandan sauce studded with small sago, or tapioca pearls. It's the perfect treat for your next get-together. The most time-consuming part of making this recipe is waiting for the gelatin to set up overnight, but it's worth your while.

* Nonstick spray
* 1½ cups young coconut water
* 1 teaspoon agar-agar powder
* ¾ cup sugar
* ½ teaspoon pandan extract
* 1 (12-ounce) jar nata de coco in syrup
* 1 (12-ounce) jar kaong in syrup
* 1½ cups unsweetened, full-fat coconut milk
* 1 (14-ounce) can sweetened condensed milk

* 3 (0.25-ounce) envelopes unflavored gelatin powder
* 1 frozen pandan leaf, thawed and tied into a knot
* ⅓ cup small sago, uncooked

*Continued*

1   Grease an 8 × 8-inch square pan with nonstick spray and line with parchment paper. You want enough overhang on all sides to be able to easily lift the gulaman out later.

2   Combine the young coconut water, agar-agar powder, and $1/2$ cup of the sugar in a small saucepan. Cook over low heat, stirring frequently with a rubber spatula, until the mixture starts to boil, 5 to 6 minutes. Let the mixture boil for another 2 minutes, then turn off the heat and stir in $1/4$ teaspoon of the pandan extract. Immediately pour the mixture into the prepared pan. Let cool to room temperature for about 20 minutes. Transfer to the fridge and chill for at least 2 hours to completely set.

3   After chilling, take the gulaman out of the square pan using the parchment paper overhang. Cut into $1/2$-inch cubes.

4   Grease a 12-cup Bundt pan with nonstick spray. Place the gulaman cubes in an even layer at the bottom of the pan.

5   Pour the nata de coco in a colander set over the kitchen sink. Give it a light stir with a wooden spoon until all the syrup is discarded. Sprinkle a layer of nata de coco in an even layer over the gulaman cubes.

6   Drain the kaong in the colander set over the kitchen sink. Sprinkle the kaong in an even layer over the nata de coco.

7   In a large bowl, whisk together 1 cup of the coconut milk, $1/2$ of the can of condensed milk, and the remaining $1/4$ cup sugar until well combined.

8   Combine the gelatin powder and $1^{1}/2$ cups water in a large measuring cup. Whisk together so the gelatin is incorporated into the water. Set aside to bloom for 5 minutes.

9   In a small saucepan, heat 1 cup water with the pandan knot over medium-high heat. Cook until the water comes to a boil, then remove the pandan knot with metal tongs. Pour the hot water into the large measuring cup and whisk the contents together until the gelatin is dissolved.

10   Quickly pour the gelatin mixture into the large bowl with the coconut milk mixture. Whisk until well combined and ladle it all into the Bundt cake mold. Transfer the pan to the fridge to chill overnight.

11   Pour 5 cups water in a medium saucepan and bring to a boil over medium-high heat. Add in the sago. Stir occasionally with a wooden spoon and simmer until the balls are mostly clear with a white center, 13 to 15 minutes.

12   Turn off the heat and cover the saucepan with a lid. Let the sago sit undisturbed until the tapioca balls are completely clear and translucent, 28 to 30 minutes. Using a large sieve, drain and rinse the sago.

13   Whisk $1/2$ cup of the coconut milk, the remaining $1/2$ of a can of condensed milk, and the remaining $1/4$ teaspoon pandan extract together in a medium bowl. Fold in the cooked sago until well combined to complete the coconut sago sauce.

14   Take the chilled jelly out of the fridge and quickly invert onto a large cake stand with a lip. Pour some of the coconut sago sauce around the base of the jelly. Serve slices with desired amount of leftover sauce. Store any leftovers in an airtight container in the fridge for up to 3 days.

# Tsokolate (Filipino Hot Chocolate) Pandesal Pudding

*Makes 24 servings*

One of my favorite ways to eat pandesal, Filipino bread rolls, is to dunk one whole in hot chocolate. My dad prefers dipping it in coffee. The bread sops up the warm drink, and it makes for a relaxing breakfast. This recipe begs the question, "What if this, but at a bigger scale?" By turning pandesal into a bread pudding with tablea, or roasted cacao tablets, for flavoring the custard, you can have a whole tray of it to share with your friends and family. You can find tablea at Filipino grocery stores, but you can alternatively use your favorite chopped chocolate instead. Broiling marshmallows on top makes this dessert even more decadent.

* 16 ounces Basic Pandesal, cut into 1-inch cubes (page 190)
* 7 ounces tablea (see page 14)
* ½ cup whole milk
* 1 cup heavy cream, cold
* 1 cup packed dark brown sugar
* ½ teaspoon kosher salt
* 1 teaspoon vanilla extract
* 4 large eggs plus 2 large egg yolks, at room temperature
* Nonstick spray
* 1 cup semisweet chocolate chips
* 3 cups Double-Toasted Coconut Marshmallows (page 91)

1   Position a rack in the middle of the oven and preheat the oven to 350°F. Line a baking sheet with a silicone mat.

2   Spread the pandesal cubes in an even layer on the lined baking sheet.

3   Bake the pandesal for 20 minutes, or until toasted and golden brown. Stir the cubes halfway through the baking time to make sure all sides get toasted.

4   Take the baking sheet out of the oven and transfer to a wire rack to cool while you make the custard.

5   Place the tablea and milk in a medium saucepan. Cook over medium-low heat, stirring frequently with a rubber spatula, until the tablea are completely dissolved in the milk, 8 to 10 minutes.

6   Pour the tsokolate mixture into a large bowl. Whisk in the heavy cream, brown sugar, salt, and vanilla. If the mixture isn't warm to the touch (if it is, wait 5 to 10 minutes), whisk in the eggs and egg yolks until the custard is smooth.

7   Add the toasted pandesal cubes and stir with a wooden spoon until well coated in the custard. Loosely cover the bowl with plastic wrap and let sit at room temperature for 40 to 45 minutes, until the cubes have mostly absorbed the custard.

8   Grease a 9 × 13-inch glass baking dish with nonstick spray. Pour the pudding into the dish. Sprinkle the surface of the pudding with chocolate chips in an even layer.

9   Bake for 40 to 45 minutes, or until the edges are set and a toothpick inserted into the center comes out clean.

10   Take the bread pudding out of the oven and sprinkle the marshmallows in an even layer on top.

11   Turn on the broiler and broil the bread pudding until the marshmallows are slightly gooey and golden brown, 3 to 6 minutes. Take the finished bread pudding out of the oven and cut the pudding into slices. Serve warm. Store the leftovers in an airtight container in the fridge for up to 4 days.

# Halo-Halo Baked Alaska

*Makes 6 servings*

If there were a Filipino dessert hall of fame, halo-halo would reign supreme. Halo-halo is a refreshing shaved ice dessert that is piled high with toppings, including but not limited to sweet beans, evaporated milk, jackfruit, and ice cream. *Halo-halo* literally means "mix-mix" in English, which is what you're supposed to do with all the ingredients.

This might be controversial, but when I was growing up, my preferred way of attacking halo-halo was to devour only my favorite bits—the ice cream and ube halaya—first. If the halo-halo featured my top-choice Filipino ice cream brand, Magnolia, I would dive right into those scoops immediately. Whenever I couldn't finish the rest, I'd hand it off to my mom to drink the melted slush. I know, I know! I'm just as bad as Tom Hanks in *You've Got Mail* when he sasses Meg Ryan by scraping all of the caviar garnish onto his plate in one fell swoop! I can't resist ice cream, and making a baked Alaska with the flavors of halo-halo is the kind of ice-cream-to-milk-and-topping ratio I've always dreamed of.

Making a halo-halo baked Alaska is quite an involved process, but don't let the horror stories from an ice cream week challenge on *The Great British Bake-Off* scare you. It's definitely doable at home and with ample time for the layers to set in the freezer. Besides ube and mango ice cream, this recipe features an evaporated milk granita steeped with jackfruit that encompasses the shaved ice aspect of halo-halo. It needs to be made the night before, but once you have enough of the frozen flakes, it is perfect as a layer along with Kapuso halo-halo fruit and bean mix. At the base of this baked Alaska, you have a tender coconut sponge cake to complement the tropical-flavored components. There are billows of Swiss meringue spread all over the frosty dome, which get torched to give the dessert its characteristic "baked" look. Serve each slice with a smattering of toasted pinipig, just like you would a traditional halo-halo.

## Evaporated Milk Granita

* 1 (20-ounce) can yellow jackfruit in syrup
* 1 (12-ounce) can evaporated milk
* ⅓ cup sugar

## Coconut Sponge Cake

* Nonstick spray
* 1 cup plus 2 tablespoons cake flour
* 1½ teaspoons baking powder
* ¼ teaspoon kosher salt
* 4 large eggs,
  at room temperature

*Continued*

* ⅓ cup whole milk, at room temperature
* ¾ teaspoon coconut extract
* ¼ cup vegetable oil
* ¾ cup sugar
* ½ teaspoon cream of tartar

## Filling

* 2¾ cups ube ice cream (Magnolia brand preferred)
* 1 (12-ounce) jar halo-halo fruit mix and beans (Kapuso brand preferred)
* 1½ cups mango ice cream (Magnolia brand preferred)

## Swiss Meringue

* 6 large egg whites, at room temperature
* ¼ teaspoon cream of tartar
* 1 cup sugar
* 3 tablespoons toasted pinipig or Rice Krispies, for topping

## Evaporated Milk Granita

1    At least one night before planning to serve the baked Alaska, drain the jackfruit using a large sieve; discard the syrup. Place the jackfruit in a medium bowl. Pour the evaporated milk over the jackfruit, cover the bowl with plastic wrap, and let it steep overnight in the fridge.

2    Take the bowl out of the fridge and strain the milk into a shallow rectangular baking dish. Squeeze out any remaining liquid from the jackfruit directly into the milk.

3    Whisk the milk with the sugar, and cover the dish with plastic wrap. Place it in the freezer. After 30 minutes of freezing, take the dish out of the freezer and scrape the frozen parts from the edges toward the center with a fork. Place it back in the freezer and repeat this process until the milk is completely frozen.

4    Store the granita in the freezer in an airtight container until you're ready to assemble the baked Alaska. This recipe will make more than what you'll need for the baked Alaska, so you can save the leftovers in the freezer for up to 1 week.

## Coconut Sponge Cake

5    Position a rack in the middle of the oven and preheat the oven to 325°F. Grease a 10 × 15-inch jelly roll pan with nonstick spray and line with parchment paper.

6    In a small bowl, mix together the cake flour, baking powder, and salt until the baking powder is evenly distributed. Set aside.

7    Separate the eggs, placing the yolks in a large bowl and the egg whites in a clean and dry medium bowl. In the large bowl, whisk the egg yolks, milk, coconut extract, vegetable oil, and ¼ cup of the sugar by hand. Slowly add in the flour mixture and continue to whisk until well combined.

8    In the medium bowl, beat the egg whites and cream of tartar with an electric hand mixer on medium-high speed until soft peaks form, 1 to 2 minutes. Gradually add in the remaining ½ cup sugar until stiff peaks form, another 1 to 2 minutes. Using a rubber spatula, gently fold the meringue into the flour mixture in three batches, mixing after each batch until the meringue is fully incorporated into the batter. Pour the batter into the lined jelly roll pan.

9    Bake for 14 to 16 minutes, or until a toothpick inserted into the center comes out clean and the

# HALO-HALO

TOASTED PINIPIG — ICE CREAM (MANGO OR UBE)

EVAPORATED MILK — SHAVED ICE

JACKFRUIT — KAONG

GULAMAN — SWEETENED BEANS (RED+WHITE)

MACAPUNO STRINGS —

top of the cake is lightly browned. Transfer the pan to a wire rack to cool completely.

10 Once cooled, cut out a 7½-inch circle of the cake. You can cut the circle out using parchment paper as a guide or with an adjustable cake ring. Feel free to eat the remaining scraps or save them for later in an airtight container at room temperature for up to 3 days.

## Filling

11 Line a 1½-quart glass bowl with plastic wrap. Scoop the ube ice cream into the bowl and create a thick wall at the base. With the back of a rubber spatula, carve out a well by smearing the center section of ice cream in a circular motion until

there is a hollow cavity. Cover the bowl with plastic wrap and freeze for 30 minutes to firm up.

12 Take the bowl out of the freezer and peel back the plastic wrap. Using a large sieve, drain the halo-halo mix and discard any excess syrup. Add ¼ cup plus 2 tablespoons of the halo-halo mix into the hollow cavity. You can store any leftover drained halo-halo mix in an airtight container in the fridge for up to 2 days. Then add ½ cup of the evaporated milk granita and spread it out in an even layer. Cover the bowl with the plastic wrap and freeze for 30 minutes to firm up.

*Continued*

**Custards, Puddings & Chilled Desserts**

**13** Take the bowl out of the freezer and peel back the plastic wrap. Top the granita layer with the mango ice cream, then flatten the ice cream so it's a smooth and flat surface. Make sure to leave at least a 1³/₄-inch-high clearance for the cake. Cover the bowl with the plastic wrap and freeze for 30 minutes to firm up.

**14** Take the bowl out of the freezer and peel back the plastic wrap. Place the cake circle on the mango ice cream layer. Cover the top of the cake with plastic wrap and freeze for at least 4 hours, preferably overnight.

### Swiss Meringue

**15** Once you're ready to serve the baked Alaska, you can start making the Swiss meringue. Bring 2 inches of water to a simmer in a medium saucepan set over medium-high heat. Combine the egg whites, cream of tartar, and sugar in a medium bowl. Set the bowl on top of the saucepan.

**16** Cook, whisking constantly, until the mixture reaches 160°F. Immediately pour the contents into the bowl of a stand mixer fitted with the whisk attachment.

**17** Whip on medium-high speed until it forms stiff peaks, 5 to 6 minutes. Let the meringue cool to room temperature before using.

**18** Remove the ice cream dome from the freezer and invert onto a 9-inch cake round and place it on a cake stand.

**19** Cover the cake with an even layer of Swiss meringue, ensuring no ice cream is showing and it is completely sealed. You can make decorative swirls with a spoon or spatula to create tiny peaks.

**20** Lightly toast the meringue with a kitchen blowtorch, 3 to 4 inches away from the cake, until evenly browned on all sides. If you don't have a blowtorch, you can alternatively place the cake under the broiler for a couple minutes to brown the meringue. Cut into six equal portions and top with ¹/₂ tablespoon of the toasted pinipig per slice. Serve immediately.

# Chai Leche Flan

*Makes 8 servings*

I would be remiss if I didn't include a leche flan recipe in this book! Although there's a wide array of renditions of this dessert from around the world, I believe Filipino leche flan is the richest of them all. I'm relieved that my dad was able to write down his recipe for me when I first released my zine, *flipped: matamis*. My friend Meghan also graciously shared her nani Ramila's chai masala recipe to incorporate into this flan. The mix of warm spices complements the sweetness of this egg custard. You can bake the leche flan in classic llaneras, the traditional oval-shaped metal pans from the Philippines, but I like using a heart-shaped aluminum pan for the cuteness of it.

## Nani's Chai Masala Mix

* I tablespoon ground black pepper
* I tablespoon ground cinnamon
* I ¹/₂ tablespoons cardamom powder
* ¹/₂ tablespoon ground nutmeg

## Leche Flan

* ³/₄ cup granulated sugar
* 10 large egg yolks
* ¹/₂ tablespoon chai masala mix (recipe above)
* I (12-ounce) can evaporated milk
* I (14-ounce) can sweetened condensed milk
* I teaspoon vanilla extract

## Nani's Chai Masala Mix

1   Whisk all the ingredients in a small bowl until all spices are evenly distributed. You will have leftovers, so store the mix in an airtight container.

## Leche Flan

2   Position a rack in the middle of the oven and preheat the oven to 350°F.

3   Place the sugar in a medium saucepan. Cook and stir frequently using a rubber spatula over low heat until the sugar is dissolved and turns golden brown, 11 to 13 minutes. Immediately pour the caramel into an 8-inch aluminum heart-shaped pan. Rotate the pan until the caramel evenly coats the whole surface. If it hardens before you cover some spots, you can hold the pan over the stovetop on low heat to melt the caramel again. Set aside as the caramel completely hardens.

*Continued*

4    In a large measuring cup, gently whisk the egg yolks, ½ tablespoon of chai masala mix, evaporated milk, condensed milk, and vanilla until smooth. Using a large sieve, slowly pour the mixture directly on top of the hardened caramel. Cover the pan with aluminum foil.

5    Place the heart-shaped pan in a larger pan or baking dish. Fill the larger pan with boiling water until it's halfway up the sides of the heart-shaped pan. I use a 9 × 13-inch aluminum cake pan for the water bath.

6    Bake for 45 to 48 minutes in the preheated oven. When the flan is fully cooked, the middle will be slightly jiggly but the sides should be set.

7    Carefully remove the heart-shaped pan from the oven and set it on a wire cooling rack. Let the flan cool to room temperature for about I hour. Once the hour is up, transfer to the fridge to chill overnight.

8    To serve, remove the aluminum foil and run a knife carefully around the edges of the flan to loosen it. Cover the surface with a plate and quickly invert it so that the flan falls onto the plate. Cut into slices and enjoy. Store any leftovers in an airtight container in the fridge for up to 3 days.

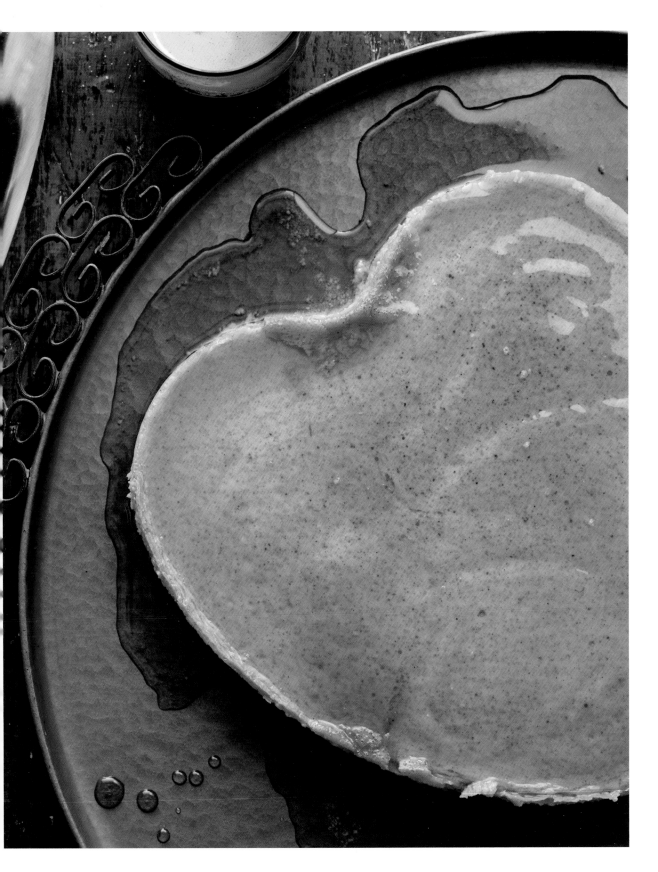

# Floating Islands with a Salted Duck Egg Crème Anglaise

*Makes 2 servings*

When I was younger, one day my parents were so excited to attempt to make brazo de Mercedes, a Filipino dessert made of baked pillowy meringue rolled in custard, at home. They even went to Michaels for a special cake comb just to decorate the edges, too. Unfortunately, it was a failed experiment for them. The meringue collapsed and the custard tasted like scrambled eggs. I remember how sad they were that it didn't turn out how they had planned. Although it was an unsuccessful bake, it inspired me to attack the dessert's elements from a different angle.

Brazo de Mercedes and floating islands are very similar because they are both chilled, light, and airy egg-based desserts. The main difference is that floating islands are meringues poached in milk and served in a pool of custard sauce. When I visited the Philippines in 2019, I saw signs advertising salted duck egg–flavored ice cream outside a store, and it made me want to add the ingredient to the vanilla bean sauce for this recipe. The addition of salted duck egg, which you can buy at any Asian supermarket already cooked, provides some more savory, gamey flavor in the custard. I usually eat these salted duck eggs as part of tomato salads seasoned with spiced vinegar. The poached meringues are topped with spun sugar nests, which you don't have to include, but they add a lot of pizzazz to the dish.

## Meringues

* 4 large egg whites, at room temperature
* ¼ teaspoon cream of tartar
* ¼ cup sugar
* 1½ cups whole milk

## Crème Anglaise

* 2 cooked salted duck eggs (see page 14)
* 4 large egg yolks, at room temperature
* ½ cup sugar

* ¼ cup heavy cream
* 1½ cups whole milk
* ½ tablespoon vanilla bean paste

## Assembly

* Nonstick spray (optional)
* ¾ cup sugar, for spun-sugar nests (optional)

*Continued*

## Meringues

**1**  Place the egg whites and cream of tartar in the bowl of a stand mixer fitted with the whisk attachment. Whip on medium-high speed until the mixture reaches soft peaks, 1 to 2 minutes.

**2**  Gradually stir in the sugar, 1 tablespoon at a time. Whip on medium-high speed until the meringue reaches stiff peaks, another 1 to 2 minutes.

**3**  Line a plate with a paper towel. Pour the milk into a medium saucepan and heat the milk to a simmer over low heat. Once the milk is simmering, scoop ¼ cup of the meringue mixture into the saucepan per island. You can poach two at a time. Cook for 2 to 3 minutes on each side. The meringues will look puffy when cooked. Using a slotted spoon, transfer the poached meringues to the lined plate. Repeat until all the meringue mixture is used up.

**4**  Let the meringues cool to room temperature, then transfer to the fridge to chill for at least 2 hours. It's normal if they shrink a bit as they cool.

## Crème Anglaise

**5**  Crack and remove the cooked salted duck eggs from their shells. Cut each in half and scoop out the yolk. Place the yolks in a small bowl and save the whites to snack on. Add the fresh egg yolks and sugar to the bowl. Whisk together until smooth. Set aside, but keep the bowl close to your stovetop.

**6**  In a medium saucepan, combine the heavy cream, whole milk, and vanilla bean paste. Cook over medium-low heat, stirring frequently with a wooden spoon, until small bubbles just appear around the edges of the pan, 4 to 5 minutes.

**7**  Ladle ¼ cup of the hot milk mixture into the egg yolk mixture and quickly whisk to temper the egg yolks. Whisk another ¼ cup of the milk mixture into the bowl, and immediately pour the mixture back into the saucepan.

**8**  Reduce the heat to low. Cook, stirring constantly with a wooden spoon, until the custard thickens enough to coat the spoon, 4 to 5 minutes. To test if it's done, dip the spoon in the mixture and trace a line across it with your finger. If it leaves a trail, it's ready to be taken off the heat.

**9**  Using a large sieve, strain the crème anglaise into a medium bowl. Immediately place a sheet of plastic wrap directly on the surface of the custard to prevent a skin from forming. Cool at room temperature for 30 minutes and then transfer to the fridge to chill for at least 2 hours.

SALTED DUCK EGG

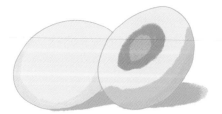

## Assembly

**10** When you're ready to serve, make the spun-sugar nests if you'd like to add them on top of your floating islands. (Feel free to skip straight to plating if you choose not to make them.) Grease a large glass bowl and two wooden spoons with nonstick spray. Set the wooden spoons about 6 inches apart from each other on top of the bowl. Set aside.

**11** Place the sugar into a medium saucepan. Cook over low heat, stirring frequently with a rubber spatula until the sugar completely melts. Clip a candy thermometer to the saucepan. Cook, stirring frequently, until the caramel turns golden brown and reaches the hard-crack stage, about 300°F. If you drop a spoonful of the syrup in cold water, it will form brittle threads that will crack if you try to pick them up. This process should take about 6 to 8 minutes. Turn off the heat.

**12** Line a baking sheet with parchment paper. Let the caramel cool in the pan for 2 to 3 minutes. To test if it's ready to be spun, dip a fork into it and pull straight up. If long threads start to form at the bottom of the fork, it's ready. Take a whisk (ideally a ball whisk) or a fork, quickly dip it in the hot caramel, and shake back and forth across the handles of the two wooden spoons. As you repeat the motion, you will start to create a network of sugar threads. Be careful not to burn yourself with the hot sugar. If the caramel in the pot hardens before you're able to finish creating threads, gently reheat it on the stove until it melts again.

**13** Once you're done, use your hands to gently gather the threads into 3-inch-wide nests. Place each finished nest on the lined baking sheet. You should have four nests total.

**14** Plate the floating islands by dividing the crème anglaise evenly between two shallow bowls. Place the poached meringues on top. Adorn with spun sugar nests and serve immediately.

# Taho Panna Cotta

*Makes 4 servings*

In the Philippines, you'll hear "Tahoooooooo!" echo throughout a neighborhood when a vendor has them for sale. I love the silky tofu layered with warm arnibal (brown sugar syrup; see page 28) and seeing sago, or chewy tapioca pearls, bobbing in the cup. For this dessert, the soft tofu panna cotta is served cold but has all the makings of a traditional taho, which includes arnibal and sago on top. Whether you're serving the panna cotta for a dinner party dessert or saving it for a sweet treat in the morning, you'll be able to enjoy it at any time of day.

* 1 (0.25-ounce) envelope unflavored gelatin powder
* 1 cup soy milk
* 1 (14-ounce) block silken tofu
* 1/2 cup sugar
* 1/4 teaspoon kosher salt
* 1/4 cup big sago, uncooked
* 1 cup Arnibal (page 28), cold

1   Line an 8 × 8-inch square pan with a kitchen towel. Place four 12-ounce glass cups in the lined pan. Tilt them facing outward at a 45-degree angle so that they are leaning against two opposite sides of the pan.

2   Combine the gelatin powder and 1/4 cup of the soy milk in a small bowl. Whisk together so the gelatin is incorporated into the milk. Set aside to bloom for 5 minutes.

3   Place the tofu in a blender and puree until smooth, 20 to 30 seconds.

4   In a medium saucepan, combine the pureed tofu, remaining 3/4 cup soy milk, the sugar, and salt. Cook over medium-high heat, stirring frequently with a rubber spatula, until the sugar is dissolved, 2 to 3 minutes.

5   Pour the gelatin mixture into the saucepan. Cook, stirring constantly, until the panna cotta mix just begins to form bubbles before boiling, 9 to 11 minutes. Remove from the heat.

*Continued*

6　Using a large sieve, strain 1 cup of the mixture into each glass. Let the panna cotta cool to room temperature for 20 minutes before carefully transferring the pan to the fridge. Chill overnight for the panna cotta to set.

7　To cook the sago, bring 4 cups water to a boil in a medium saucepan over medium-high heat. Add the sago, stirring occasionally with a wooden spoon, for 30 minutes. Remove from the heat and drain the sago in a large sieve.

8　Add 4 cups fresh water to the saucepan and repeat this boiling and straining process again.

9　For the third round, boil the sago for 30 minutes as usual, but do not strain the water. Turn off the heat and cover the pan with a lid. The sago will still have white centers. Let the sago sit in the pan overnight.

10　The following day, strain and rinse the sago. The balls should be fully translucent and no longer hard. If there are still some white centers, boil 4 cups water over medium-high heat and boil the sago for another 5 to 10 minutes. Strain and rinse the sago again. Place in a small bowl.

11　Take the chilled panna cotta out of the fridge. Fill each glass with equal portions of the cooked sago and chilled arnibal syrup before serving. Store any leftovers covered in plastic wrap in the fridge for up to 2 days.

# Pass the Pasalubong

I used to think that having it together meant that I could prep a week's worth of meals, and that I knew how to read a book on the subway and not miss a single transfer. By these standards, I didn't have it together before and especially after March 2020. When my company pivoted to working at home full-time, I was filled with a sense of dread. I wondered when we'd ever return to the way things were. Would I lose my job because no one could go to concerts anymore? When would there be a vaccine widely available? I was in a pit of despair worrying if I'd ever see my parents again. Or even worse, that they'd get sick with a virus there was no cure for. Once the panic just became a part of daily life, I began to turn to Filipino food for comfort.

It dawned on me that I couldn't just go through life depending on quarterly pilgrimages to Jollibee for Filipino spaghetti sweetened with banana ketchup. It was no longer viable to visit my family in Jersey, where they'd always have Philippine Bread House's fluffy pandan chiffon cake. I was hit with a sense of urgency to preserve my culture through food. I avoided going to out-of-the-way stores, which meant that I relied on buying groceries online. Luckily, more services cropped up that shipped Filipino ingredients to your door. Instead of solely relying on takeout to have a morsel of adobo or kare-kare, I was cooking it at home. By FaceTiming my parents anytime I stirred a vat of coconut cream that split into oil and the toasted curds called latik, I could ask them over live video if the latik was dark enough to take off the heat. I used to be so nervous to cook or bake anything Filipino because I knew it wouldn't turn out exactly like my parents' dishes. The moment I accepted that was true and it didn't mean that what I was making was necessarily worse than their versions–just different–it was so liberating. At least trying to make it was better than not doing so at all. Working from home also provided more hours in the day to marinate meat and break up baking projects into feasible chunks.

In the summer of 2020, I was itching to engage with my local community in more ways than just scrolling through Instagram infographics. Besides attending Black Lives Matter protests, I wanted to contribute my skills to the cause too. I noticed Bakers Against Racism was doing incredible work with bake sales across the country benefiting mutual aid organizations. Seeing people do this in real time made me think I could do the same. I ordered a kakanin box from my friend Jessica in July, which she had available for pickup and delivery in Brooklyn. Not only did the rice cakes taste amazing, I admired that she was able to donate profits toward bail funds in the Philippines and resources for the Black trans community. I was inspired to do my own treat boxes, and launch my own baking blog in tandem with it.

I'd had the domain and social media handles reserved for *The Dusky Kitchen* since December 2019. I was invigorated by traveling to the Philippines that winter, so the first thing I wanted to do when I got back to New York was lean into my love of baking again. Originally, I was going to talk about what I baked during dusk whenever I'd come home from work. In my apartment in Bed-Stuy, which I shared with three other roommates, there was only one window in the kitchen. I thought the working title, *The Dusky Kitchen*, would be a quirky spin on this otherwise annoying problem of lack of natural light for food photography. Did I touch WordPress between then and July 2020? I did not. As I like to say when projects fall through,

life just got in the way. When the world comes to a standstill, you have a lot of time to reflect on yourself and how you want to spend your days. I revived my logins as soon as I said to myself that I wanted to write recipes to go along with each dessert in the treat box. That way, people outside of New York City who couldn't buy a box could try my recipes in their own kitchens.

Using inspiration from childhood memories, I made a Filipino American fusion dessert menu with ingredients like ube extract, pork floss, and glutinous rice flour that I got delivered from Asian grocery stores. I had to make sure that these recipes would transport well and that I could scale them up to make at least four dozen boxes. Since I was missing the fried peach mango pies from my local Jollibee, I riffed off the flavors for a baked hand pie iteration. I was excited to experiment with sweet and salty combinations for a dessert like my pork floss and white miso brownies. When I was craving the ube puto just like the ones my family used to buy at the Goldilocks by Auntie Flor's house in San Jose, I steamed some of these purple rice cakes and topped them with grated Cheddar. I tested the recipes for about a month before I made an official announcement. I called the treat box pasalubong as an ode to the souvenirs I'd bring back from the motherland to my friends and family. When I announced the treat box on Instagram and Twitter, the response was resounding joy and excitement. People who weren't just my boyfriend, Jason, and my roommates wanted to try my strawberry polvoron (page 141) and Horchata Bibingka (page 41). Two days later, food writer Emma Orlow published a *Time Out* article about the pasalubong boxes, and they sold out within the week.

Creating a baking schedule for that drop was mayhem! On top of the logistics of finalizing a delivery route and communicating with people who ordered, buying enough groceries to make 288 desserts for forty-eight boxes was challenging as someone who'd never made such huge quantities before. Working full-time, albeit remotely, proved another challenge to have enough hours to do all the actual baking by myself. I took the Friday off to dedicate my time to baking and was in the kitchen nonstop from then on until Sunday of the big day.

I roped in Jason to drive the finished boxes and me to Fort Greene Park for pickups. Sitting underneath a tree with mysterious gray tubs filled with desserts looked like some clandestine operation, but people still swung by to grab their boxes. For the first time since the start of the pandemic, I was interacting with people outside of my apartment, and I relished getting to know them. As soon as the pickup window ended, Jason and I raced back to the car to complete the deliveries to apartments across Brooklyn, Manhattan, and Queens. After all was said and done, I was able to donate 100 percent of all the proceeds to Bed-Stuy Strong, a mutual aid network right in my neighborhood.

Throughout the course of 2020 and 2021, I continued adding more rounds of pasalubong treat boxes with coordinating recipe blog posts. When I did Christmas cookie tins, I remember standing out in the frigid cold and passing them out to people with my teeth chattering and a soggy checklist in hand. I organized pasalubong pickups in heat, rain, sleet, and snow before eventually migrating to doing them indoors at my local wine bar, Tailfeather. To date, I've donated over eight thousand dollars and baked over two thousand desserts for mutual aid. Not only was it incredibly rewarding to see people enjoy my creations, I really felt like I was making a difference in others' lives. The money made from selling my treat boxes went to providing typhoon relief in the Philippines, assisting mom-and-pop restaurant owners in New York City's Chinatown whose businesses were suffering in the wake of COVID-19, and helping fund neighbor-led volunteer initiatives in Brooklyn and Queens. No matter how tiring it was to make desserts at such high volumes, I felt like I learned so much each time and elevated my skills as a baker.

# Milky Avocado Ice Pops

*Makes 7 ice pops*

One of my favorite comfort watches is *The Princess Diaries*. There's a scene where Anne Hathaway's character, Mia Thermopolis, unknowingly takes a large bite of green sorbet and makes a ruckus about how cold it is. For years, I thought that green sorbet was avocado-flavored! (That theory of mine has been debunked—it was supposedly a mint sorbet.) Since avocados are commonly used in desserts in the Philippines, I've always been fond of any sweet avocado recipes. I remember sitting at the kitchen table while my parents mixed together bowls of shaved ice, ripe avocado flesh, and sweetened milk. I wanted to make ice pops inspired by this dessert our family loves so much. For these ice pops, using Greek yogurt makes them a tad sour, but the acid also helps keep the avocado from browning.

* 1 ripe avocado
* 1 cup plain Greek yogurt
* 1 (14-ounce) can sweetened condensed milk

1   Cut the avocado in half, remove the pit, and scoop out the flesh into a blender. Add the Greek yogurt and sweetened condensed milk. Blitz until the mixture is smooth, 1 to 2 minutes.

2   Spoon the mixture into steel or silicone ice pop molds until filled up to the top. Place the cover over them and then insert an ice pop stick in each mold. Freeze for at least 4 hours, preferably overnight. When ready to serve, run the molds under hot water for about 10 seconds to easily remove the ice pops. Store any leftovers in an airtight container in the freezer for up to 3 weeks.

# Tibok-Tibok for One

### *Makes 1 serving*

Tibok-tibok is a Kapampangan pudding traditionally made with carabao milk and topped with latik, or toasted coconut curds. When my parents lived in Pampanga, they loved pouring fresh carabao milk over rice and eating it with tuyo, salted dried fish, on top for breakfast. Carabao, or water buffalo, milk has a higher fat content than cow milk, which results in a rich and creamy tibok-tibok. *Tibok-tibok*'s literal meaning is "heartbeat," which is what the pudding resembles as it finishes cooking. Large bubbles rise to the surface in what appears to be a pulsating mixture!

You'll usually find tibok-tibok served at fiestas in large servings for sharing with family and friends. I came up with this recipe for those of us who crave this decadent dessert but maybe live alone or don't have the fridge space for a giant tray of it. Sometimes, you just want a mug's worth of tibok-tibok in the middle of the night just because. While it's ideal to have fresh carabao milk on hand, it can be hard to source if there are no local farms in your area that carry it. You can replace carabao milk with whole cow milk instead.

* 1¼ cups fresh carabao milk (see page 13) or whole cow milk
* 2 tablespoons rice flour
* ¼ cup sugar
* 1 tablespoon Latik (Toasted Coconut Curds, page 30), for topping, plus more as desired

1. Combine ¼ cup of the carabao milk with the rice flour in a small bowl. Whisk to dissolve any clumps. Set aside.

2. In a small saucepan, stir the remaining 1 cup carabao milk and the sugar with a wooden spoon. Cook over low heat, stirring occasionally, until the sugar is dissolved, 1 to 2 minutes.

3. Add in the rice flour mixture and continue to stir occasionally until the pudding reaches a boil, 5 to 6 minutes.

4. Pour the pudding into a 10- or 12-ounce mug and immediately press plastic wrap on top of the pudding to prevent a film from forming on the surface. Chill the mug of tibok-tibok in the fridge for at least 2 hours, so it's completely set.

5. Before serving, sprinkle the latik on top of the pudding. I like to have extra latik on hand to have some with every bite. If you have any leftovers, cover the mug with plastic wrap and store in the fridge for up to 3 days.

# Fiesta Fruit Salad

### *Makes 8 servings*

Nothing screams party to me more than fruit salad. There is always a giant vat of the creamy fruit cocktail mix at my family's celebrations. I've heard murmurs of American ambrosia salad over the years bearing some resemblance to it, but Filipino fruit salad certainly doesn't contain marshmallows. Filipino fruit salad does have chewy ingredients like nata de coco, or coconut gel, and kaong, or sugar palm fruit, which you can find at your local Filipino grocery store. The biggest difference between my fruit salad recipe and my parents' is the canned fruit selection. I have the strongest aversions toward canned pears and maraschino cherries (they taste so mushy and medicine-like to me!), so I opted for refreshing fruits that I prefer instead, like canned lychee and grapefruit.

* I (15.25-ounce) can peach chunks in syrup
* I (19.9-ounce) can peeled and pitted lychees in syrup
* I (20-ounce) can pineapple chunks in syrup
* I (15-ounce) can red grapefruit in syrup
* I (12-ounce) jar kaong in syrup
* I (12-ounce) jar nata de coco in syrup
* I (14-ounce) can sweetened condensed milk
* I cup heavy cream, cold

1   Pour the peach chunks, lychees, pineapple chunks, red grapefruit, kaong, and nata de coco in a colander set over the kitchen sink. Give all the fruits a light stir with a wooden spoon until all the syrup is discarded. Place the drained fruit mixture into a large bowl.

2   In a large measuring cup, whisk the condensed milk and heavy cream together until smooth. Pour over the fruit mixture and gently stir until evenly distributed. Cover the bowl with a lid and chill in the fridge for at least 4 hours, preferably overnight.

3   Serve cold and store any leftovers in the fridge in an airtight container for up to 5 days.

# Miso Caramelized White Chocolate Champorado with Pork Floss

*Makes 1 serving*

While traditional champorado, a sweet rice pudding, gets its chocolate flavor from the Filipino roasted cacao tablets called tablea, we never could find it at the Food 4 Less grocery store in my neighborhood. For breakfast, Lola Undi used to make champorado for my sister and me using chocolate Nesquik powder instead. Her champorado felt like a warm hug, and I'm excited to share my version, which features a different type of chocolate and topping that I find so comforting. For the chocolate, I use Valrhona Dulcey feves, which taste like caramelized white chocolate and pair exceptionally well with salty pork floss and miso. If you can't find Dulcey feves near you, feel free to substitute butterscotch chips. Pork floss is a Chinese dried, shredded meat that makes this dish feel akin to having a bowl of congee. The miso is Japanese fermented soybean paste that gives the champorado more of an umami edge.

* ½ cup uncooked glutinous rice
* 1½ teaspoons white miso paste
* 3 ounces Dulcey feves or ½ cup butterscotch chips
* Milk of your choice, for topping
* 2 tablespoons pork floss

1  In a small bowl, wash the glutinous rice with cold water and keep rinsing until the water runs clear. Using a large sieve, drain the water from the rice and place the rice in a medium saucepan.

2  Add 2 cups water, the white miso paste, and Dulcey feves to the saucepan. Cook over medium-high heat, stirring occasionally with a wooden spoon, until the mixture comes to a boil, 5 to 6 minutes.

3  Reduce the heat to low. Simmer, stirring constantly, until the mixture thickens to an oatmeal-like consistency, 12 to 15 minutes.

4  Ladle the champorado into a bowl. Pour a swirl of milk on top and serve warm with the pork floss. Store any leftover champorado in an airtight container in the fridge for up to 3 days.

# Rice Coffee Tiramisu

*Makes 9 squares*

Tiramisu is one of my favorite Italian desserts. The whipped mascarpone cream makes the ladyfingers so soft and sweet. I don't even mind that the tiny sponge cakes are soaked in black coffee, which is a beverage I find too bitter for my taste. Since I'm not the biggest coffee person, I wanted the opportunity to try making it with kapeng bigas, a Filipino roasted rice coffee. It's made by toasting raw jasmine rice and steeping it in hot water. The resulting liquid has all the nutty and smoky flavor, but none of the caffeine of actual coffee.

* 2 tablespoons raw jasmine rice
* 4 large egg yolks
* ½ cup sugar
* 3 tablespoons dark rum
* ¼ teaspoon kosher salt
* 8 ounces mascarpone cheese, at room temperature
* 1⅓ cups heavy cream, cold
* 24 ladyfingers
* 1 tablespoon unsweetened cocoa powder

1   Place the rice in a small saucepan. Cook over low heat, stirring frequently with a wooden spoon, until the rice turns a dark brown color, nearly black, 7 to 10 minutes. Transfer the toasted rice to a medium measuring cup.

2   Pour 1½ cups water into the small saucepan and bring to a boil. Pour the boiling water over the toasted rice and let the rice steep for 5 to 7 minutes, until the water has a dark brown hue to match the toasted rice.

3   Using a small sieve, strain the coffee into a small bowl. Discard the rice. Set the rice coffee aside to cool to room temperature.

4   Add 2 inches of water to a medium saucepan and bring to a simmer over medium-high heat. Have ready a large bowl filled with ice water. Combine the egg yolks, ¼ cup plus 2 tablespoons of the sugar, the rum, and salt in a medium bowl. Place the bowl on top of the saucepan. Cook, whisking constantly, until the mixture reaches 160°F and is thick, foamy, and pale yellow, about

10 minutes. Immediately transfer the medium bowl to the ice-water bowl. Let the custard cool down for 5 to 6 minutes, until it reaches room temperature.

5  Remove the medium bowl from its ice water bath. Using a rubber spatula, fold the softened mascarpone cheese into the custard until well combined.

6  Pour the heavy cream into a large bowl. Using an electric hand mixer, whip the cream on medium-high speed until soft peaks form, about 1 minute. Gradually add the remaining 2 tablespoons granulated sugar. Whip until stiff peaks form, 1 to 2 minutes. In two batches, gently fold the mascarpone mixture into the whipped cream until well combined.

7  To assemble the tiramisu, quickly dip both sides of 12 ladyfingers, one at a time, in the rice coffee and arrange them in an even layer at the bottom of an 8 × 8-inch square pan. Be careful not to dip for too long or the ladyfingers will start to disintegrate. Take half of the cream mixture and spread in an even layer over the ladyfingers. Quickly dip the other 12 ladyfingers, one at a time, in the rice coffee and arrange them on top of the cream layer.

8  Transfer the second half of the cream mixture into a piping bag fitted with a large round tip. Pipe the cream in even rows to cover the surface of the ladyfingers. Cover the pan with plastic wrap and transfer to the fridge to chill for at least 4 hours, preferably overnight.

9  When ready to serve, use a small sieve to dust the top with the cocoa powder. Cut into 9 squares. Store any leftovers in an airtight container in the fridge for up to 2 days.

# Malted Milk Maja Blanca with Corn Chip Crunch

*Makes 24 servings*

My mom's maja blanca is her signature dessert at every family gathering. Maja blanca is a Filipino coconut milk and corn pudding that is served cold. During the mornings before we'd head out to San Jose, I'd see her painstakingly stir a pot full of maja blanca over the stovetop. If I wasn't helping her with stirring the actual pudding, I'd be relegated to toasting the sweetened coconut flakes. I tinkered around with her famous recipe below by adding the malted milk powder while it's bubbling on the stove and a Frito corn chip toffee on top of the finished pudding for added flavor and texture. The malted milk powder gives the pudding a nuttiness that reminds me of malted milk shakes at old-fashioned ice cream parlors. Coating Fritos in a toffee and breaking them into bits provides a crunch in an otherwise very soft dessert.

* Nonstick spray
* 1 (16-ounce) bag frozen sweet yellow corn kernels
* 1 cup cornstarch
* 1 cup whole milk
* 4 cups unsweetened, full-fat coconut milk
* 1 (14-ounce) can sweetened condensed milk
* 1 cup malted milk powder
* 1/2 cup granulated sugar
* 1/4 teaspoon kosher salt
* 8 tablespoons (1 stick) unsalted butter
* 1/2 cup packed dark brown sugar
* 1 teaspoon vanilla extract
* 2 1/2 cups Fritos Corn Chips

1    Grease a 9 × 13-inch glass baking dish with nonstick spray. Set aside.

2    Take the bag of corn out of the freezer and massage the bag to break up any solid chunks.

3    Whisk the cornstarch and whole milk in a medium bowl until the cornstarch is dissolved.

4    In a large pot, combine the coconut milk, condensed milk, malted milk powder, granulated sugar, and salt. Cook over medium-high heat, stirring occasionally with a wooden spoon until the mixture comes to a boil, 10 to 12 minutes. Stir in the corn and cook until the mixture comes to a boil again.

5    Reduce the heat to low and then pour the cornstarch mixture into the pot. Stir constantly

*Continued*

until the mixture has the consistency of thick pudding and starts bubbling, 2 to 3 minutes. Quickly transfer the maja blanca mixture to the prepared baking dish. Cool at room temperature for 30 minutes and then cover with foil. Transfer the maja blanca to the fridge to chill for at least 2 hours.

6   While the maja blanca is chilling, make the Frito toffee. Line a baking sheet with parchment paper and set aside.

7   In a medium saucepan, combine the butter, brown sugar, and vanilla. Cook over medium-high heat, stirring frequently with a rubber spatula, until the mixture just begins to simmer, 4 to 6 minutes. Reduce the heat to low and clip a candy thermometer to the saucepan. Cook, stirring constantly until it reaches the soft-crack stage, between 270°F to 290°F. If you take a spoonful of the syrup and drop it into a small bowl of cold water, you should be able to pull it between your fingers and see it form firm but pliable threads. This can take 12 to 15 minutes. Turn off the heat.

8   Immediately stir in the Fritos until evenly coated.

9   Pour the Frito toffee onto the lined baking sheet to harden and cool to room temperature, 15 to 20 minutes. Once cooled, use a meat tenderizer or rolling pin to break the Frito toffee into bite-size pieces.

10   To serve the maja blanca, cut into squares or use a cookie cutter to cut out shapes. Sprinkle the tops with Frito toffee right before serving. Store any leftovers in an airtight container in the fridge for up to 3 days.

# Mommy's Ginataang Bilo-Bilo

*Makes 4 servings*

Ever since I was little, I've called my mom "Mommy" and dad "Daddy." I'm in my late twenties now, and I feel like I'll call them that even when I'm in my late sixties. When I used to watch *The Simpsons*, my parents were aghast that Bart would call Homer by his first name. Honorifics and all other forms of showing respect are of the utmost importance in Filipino culture. It's second nature to call all elders "Auntie" and "Uncle" because of my parents.

This recipe is for Mommy and a dessert that she loves. Ginataang bilo-bilo is a coconut soup chock-full of tropical fruits and chewy glutinous rice balls. As much as I enjoy riffing on classics, there weren't elements in this ginataang bilo-bilo that I felt compelled to tweak. Besides swapping the traditional saba bananas for plantains, I believe it's Mommy-approved.

## Sago

* ¹⁄₂ cup small sago, uncooked

## Bilo-Bilo

* ¹⁄₂ cup glutinous rice flour
* ¹⁄₄ teaspoon ube extract

## Assembly

* 1 (13.5-ounce) can unsweetened, full-fat coconut milk
* ¹⁄₄ cup plus 2 tablespoons sugar
* ¹⁄₂ teaspoon kosher salt
* 4 ounces peeled and ¹⁄₂-inch diced Japanese sweet potato
* 4 ounces peeled and ¹⁄₂-inch sliced ripe yellow plantain
* ¹⁄₂ cup drained and julienned canned yellow jackfruit

## Sago

1    Pour 6 cups water into a medium saucepan and bring to a boil over medium-high heat.

2    Add the sago. Stir occasionally with a wooden spoon and simmer until the balls are mostly clear with a white center, 13 to 15 minutes.

3    Turn off the heat and cover the saucepan with a lid. Let the sago sit undisturbed for 28 to 30 minutes, or until the tapioca balls are completely clear and translucent.

4    Using a large sieve, drain and rinse the sago. Place in a medium bowl. Pour 2 cups fresh water into the bowl for the sago to sit in while you make the soup.

*Continued*

### Bilo-Bilo

5  Place the glutinous rice flour in a small bowl.

6  In a small measuring cup, whisk together ¼ cup water and the ube extract. Add the mixture to the glutinous rice flour.

7  Mix the flour and ube water with your hands until it turns into a pliable dough, 4 to 5 minutes. Form teaspoon-size balls and place on a plate. You should end up with 20 balls. Set aside.

### Assembly

8  In a medium saucepan, combine 1½ cups water, the coconut milk, sugar, and salt. Cook, stirring occasionally, over medium-high heat until it reaches a boil, 6 to 7 minutes.

9  Add the sweet potato and reduce the heat to medium-low. Stir occasionally with a wooden spoon and simmer for 5 minutes.

10  Add the rice balls and plantain slices. Cook, stirring frequently, until the rice balls are fully cooked, another 3 to 5 minutes. The balls should float to the surface when they are done.

11  Drain the water from your bowl of sago and add the sago to the soup. Stir in the jackfruit and let it simmer until the fruit is all cooked, another 2 to 4 minutes. The sweet potato pieces should be fork-tender. Serve warm. Store any leftovers in an airtight container in the fridge for up to 3 days. You can reheat a small bowl's worth of bilo-bilo in a microwave for 1 to 2 minutes, or until it's hot enough for your liking.

# Sago't Gulaman Iced Coffee

## Makes 1 serving

I'm no coffee aficionado, but my boyfriend, Jason, sure is. He loves it as much as Agent Dale Cooper in *Twin Peaks*. After one too many all-nighters during my college years at Cal, the jitters I got from downing copious amounts of Peet's Coffee scarred me for life. I will enjoy a sweet coffee once in a blue moon, so this sago't gulaman version helps the bitter drink go down smoother. Sago't gulaman is a refreshing Filipino beverage made up of tapioca pearls, jelly cubes, and brown sugar syrup. By freezing arnibal (brown sugar syrup) into ice cubes, you get more of the flavor as it melts. I love the texture of the chewy sago and jellylike gulaman as well.

* ½ cup Arnibal (page 28)
* 2 tablespoons big sago, uncooked
* Nonstick spray
* 1 teaspoon agar-agar powder
* ½ cup sugar
* 1 cup cold-brew coffee
* Heavy cream or milk, as desired

1  Pour the arnibal into silicone ice cube molds. I like using molds with fun shapes like hearts and stars. Place in the freezer and allow to chill for at least 2 hours, or until completely frozen.

2  Add 2 cups water to a small saucepan and bring to a boil over medium-high heat. Once the water is boiling, add in the uncooked sago. Cook, stirring occasionally with a wooden spoon, for 30 minutes. Remove from the heat and strain using a large sieve. Add 2 cups of fresh water to the saucepan and repeat this boiling and straining process again.

3  For the third round, boil the sago for 30 minutes as usual, but do not strain the water. Turn off the heat and cover the pan with a lid. The sago will still have white centers. Let the sago sit overnight in the pan. After the sago is done soaking, strain and rinse the sago. The balls should be fully translucent and no longer hard. If there are still some white centers, boil 2 cups of water again and boil the sago for another 5 to 10 minutes. Strain and rinse the sago again. Place in a small bowl.

4  Grease an 8 × 8-inch square pan with nonstick spray and line with parchment paper. You want enough overhang on all sides to be able to easily lift the gulaman out later.

5  Combine 1½ cups water, the agar-agar powder, and sugar in a small saucepan. Cook over medium-low heat, stirring frequently with a rubber spatula, until the mixture starts to boil, 5 to 6 minutes. Let the mixture boil for another 2 minutes, then turn off the heat. Immediately

pour the mixture into the prepared pan. Let cool to room temperature for about 20 minutes. Transfer to the fridge and chill for at least 2 hours to completely set.

6    After chilling, take the gulaman out of the square pan using the parchment paper overhang. Cut into ½-inch cubes. You will have leftovers, so you can store them in an airtight container in the fridge for up to 4 days.

7    Place the cooked sago and 2 tablespoons of the gulaman cubes at the bottom of a glass cup. Pour in the cold-brew coffee and a touch of cream or milk, if desired. Top with arnibal ice cubes. Give it a stir and drink with a straw. Use a spoon to scoop up and eat the sago and gulaman.

# Melon Chicharron Crumble

### *Makes 6 servings*

**Chicharron, or pork rinds, were always a staple in my parents' pantry. Whenever relatives would come to visit, we'd pop open a bag to serve with a dip of spiced vinegar called saw-sawan. For this crumble, I use juicy cantaloupe and crushed-up chicharron for a porky punch of flavor. A play on melon and prosciutto, this dish is a unique sweet and savory combo that will definitely wow your friends. If you so choose, you can serve the crumble with vanilla ice cream and fresh mint leaves on top.**

* Nonstick spray
* 2 pounds cantaloupe without the rind and seeds, cut into I-inch cubes (about I³/₄ small cantaloupes)
* ¹/₃ cup granulated sugar
* ¹/₄ teaspoon kosher salt
* 2 tablespoons fresh lemon juice
* 3 tablespoons cornstarch
* I teaspoon ground cinnamon
* I teaspoon vanilla extract
* ³/₄ cup all-purpose flour
* ¹/₂ cup chicharron crumbs
* ¹/₂ cup packed dark brown sugar
* I teaspoon baking powder
* 6 tablespoons unsalted butter, cold, cut into tablespoon-size pieces
* Vanilla ice cream, for serving (optional)
* Fresh mint leaves, for garnish (optional)

1   Grease a 2-quart Dutch oven or baking dish with nonstick spray. Position a rack in the middle of the oven and preheat the oven to 375°F.

2   In a large saucepan, combine the cantaloupe, granulated sugar, salt, lemon juice, cornstarch, cinnamon, and vanilla. Cook the mixture over low heat, stirring frequently with a wooden spoon, until the fruit is softened and slightly thickened, 7 to 10 minutes. Turn off the heat and transfer the mixture to the Dutch oven. Set aside.

3   With your hands, mix the all-purpose flour, chicharron crumbs, brown sugar, and baking powder together on a silicone mat. Using a pastry cutter, cut the cold butter pieces into the dry ingredients until the mixture forms large crumbs, 4 to 6 minutes. Sprinkle the crumble topping evenly over the surface of the melon filling.

4   Bake uncovered for 30 to 35 minutes, or until the fruit juices are bubbling and the crumble topping is golden brown. Let stand for 10 to 15 minutes before serving warm. You can serve with scoops of vanilla ice cream and fresh mint leaves on top. The crumble is best eaten the day of.

# GLOSSARY

**408**: San Jose area code

**Ading (used before a name)**: Ilocano title used before a younger friend's or sibling's name

**Arnibal**: caramelized sugar syrup

**Ate (used before a name)**: honorific added for an older sister, other relative, or friend

**Bagoong Alamang**: fermented shrimp paste

**"Bahay Kubo"**: literally translates to "Cube House," an old Filipino folk song for kids

**Balikbayan**: literally translates to "return home," which refers to Filipinos coming back to the Philippines after living abroad

**Bilo-bilo**: rice balls; refers to the larger dish that is a sweet coconut soup cooked with these

**Brazo de Mercedes**: Filipino dessert composed of a meringue roll and a custard filling; literally means "Arm of Our Lady of Mercy"

**Buchi**: fried glutinous rice balls filled with red bean paste and covered in sesame seeds; adapted from the Chinese pastry jian dui

**Carabao**: water buffalo native to the Philippines; also another name for Manila mangoes

**Champorado**: sweet Filipino breakfast porridge that is typically chocolate-flavored

**Chichirya**: junk food, snacks

**Chismis**: gossip

**Dinuguan**: Filipino stew made of pork blood and intestines

**Ginataang**: to cook with coconut milk

**Gulaman**: Filipino term for agar-agar, a seaweed ingredient similar to gelatin used for making jelly desserts; also refers to the finished jelly

**Halaya**: jam

**Handaan**: feast

**Kakanin**: an umbrella term for Filipino rice cakes

**Kamias**: tree sorrel

**Kaong**: chewy, sweet palm fruit that is typically used in halo-halo

**Kuya (used before a name)**: honorific added for an older brother, other relative, or friend

**Latik**: toasted coconut curds

**Llaneras**: oval shaped pans used for making leche flan

**Lolo/Lola**: grandfather/grandmother

**Macapuno**: coconut sport; the gelatinous and soft endosperm of a special type of coconut commonly used in Filipino desserts

**Manong**: Ilocano word for "older brother" that commonly refers to the first generation of Filipinos who immigrated to the United States

**Mayumu**: Kapampangan word meaning "sweet"

**Morena**: dark-skinned Filipino woman

**Nata de coco**: sweet coconut gel produced from fermenting coconut water

**Neverías:** Mexican ice cream shops

**OFW:** Overseas Filipino Worker; a term to describe Filipinos living and working in another country

**Paleterías:** Mexican ice pop shops

**Pancit:** Filipino noodle dish

**Pandan:** screwpine leaves

**Parol:** Filipino Christmas lanterns made of tissue paper

**Pasalubong:** souvenirs or gifts typically brought from one's travels to give to friends and family

**Patis:** fish sauce

**Regla:** menstruation

**Sago:** chewy tapioca balls

**Sapin-sapin:** a layered Filipino rice cake; literally means "layer-layer"

**Sawsawan:** spiced vinegar sauce typically used for dipping fried foods in; general term for dipping sauces

**Sisig:** Kapampangan dish that consists of pork belly and pig's face with onions and chili peppers

**Swagapino:** Internet slang term for a Filipino American with street fashion sense encompassing both "swag" and "Filipino" that grew in popularity with memes on Tumblr in the early 2010s

**Tablea:** roasted cacao tablets typically used to make tsokolate and champorado

**Taho:** Filipino dessert layered with warm sugar syrup, tofu, and sago

**Teleseryes:** Filipino soap operas

**TFC:** The Filipino Channel

**Tsokolate:** Filipino hot chocolate

**Turon:** Filipino dessert or snack that is typically composed of saba banana and jackfruit rolled in a spring roll wrapper, deep fried, and then coated in a caramel sugar

**Tuyo:** salted, dried fish

**Ube:** Filipino purple yam

**Ulam:** main dish that is accompanied with a side of rice or noodles

**Utang na loob:** Filipino sense of obligation to repay one's debts, especially to one's family

Adobo Chocolate Chip
Cookies (page 143)

# ACKNOWLEDGMENTS

**T**hank you to my wonderful agent, Emmy Nordstrom Higdon! Without you, none of this would be possible. You plucked me out of obscurity from a random tweet, and your confidence in me really helped me believe that my story was worthy of telling. I am so grateful to have such a passionate agent in my corner. Thank you for having me at Westwood Creative Artists, where I am among extraordinary talent.

Sarah Kwak, thank you for being my editor and playing a pivotal role in bringing *Mayumu* to life. Your care and attention to detail, and overall expertise in the publishing industry have been so helpful to a first-time author like me. Out of all the editors who came across my proposal, you have done nothing but support my vision and reinforce that my recipes should be immortalized in print. I always knew that my book was in good hands with you and the rest of the wonderful people at Harvest. Shelby Peak, Mumtaz Mustafa, Leah Carlson-Stanisic, Kimberly Kiefer, Francesca Carlos, and April Roberts, thank for your respective talents in production editorial, cover design, interior design, production, marketing, and publicity.

To my cookbook shoot team, thank you for making sure that my desserts are shown in the best light. I could not be happier to have this opportunity to work with you all. It really did feel like summer camp, and by the end of it, I didn't want it to be over. Nico Schinco, thank you for being a fantastic photographer and letting us use your apartment as our studio. I cannot thank you and Maia George enough for making sure each shot was perfect. Kaitlin Wayne and Joy Cho, thank you both for baking and styling my desserts with the utmost care and precision. Thank you for having faith in my recipes, and showing me the kind of prowess in the kitchen that inspires me to keep going. Maeve Sheridan, thank you for sourcing the most amazing props and surfaces. In just a couple Zoom calls, you were able to see my vision and figure out how to embody my personality with stunning kitchenware I wish I could have kept in my own collection. Thank you for your dedication to make my debut cookbook as beautiful as possible. Shannon Alessandroni, thank you again for being a good pal and hand modeling on set for a day!

To my friend and illustrator, Charisse Celestial, thank you for creating the wonderful art to accompany my words and the photographs. You are my favorite artist, and I am so excited that the world gets to see your illustrations in print. Being able to work on this with you has been a Flash Thrive dream come true.

Mommy, Daddy, Argeli, and Ginelle, thank you for dealing with me when I was a really emo teen. I appreciate the space you've given me to live my best life. I'm able to accomplish all the things I've always wanted to do because of your unconditional love. And to my extended family, which stretches across California and the Philippines, you have my whole heart.

Special thank-you to Uncle Tan, Auntie Tess, Anna, and JB. Whenever I needed to run away from New York, I'd hop on the NJ Transit to stay with you. Thank you for letting me keep my winter clothes in your basement, for feeding me so much that I needed to waddle back home from Sushi Palace, and for going to every one of my pasalubong treat box pickups.

Anjile An, I think our journeys in New York are inseparable from each other, and I am so grateful that you have been my best friend every step of the way. From Keki cheesecake pick-me-ups to spontaneous concerts (and even painstakingly cutting nata de coco in tiny pieces for the cookbook shoot!), I don't want to imagine my last five-plus years without you. Thank you and your parents for supporting me with this book, and I cannot wait to hang out together in Vancouver sometime soon.

To my other friends at Cal who made dead weeks and the rest of life after that bearable, thank you, Yensy Zetino, Michelle Li, Savannah Portillo Heap, Lauren Ahn, Patty Reddi, Ilaf Esuf, Miya Singer, Meghan Babla, Amy Goodman, Jonahluis Galvez, Justin Lasola, and Keizzel Camacho. Go Bears!

To my PAAmily, Ate Molly, Ate Sydney, Ate Justine, Michael, Ading Kristina, Ading Carissa, and Ading Camille, thank you for enriching my life with your presence. You made me feel so at home in Berkeley, and I'm grateful that our bonds have lasted well beyond our college years.

Throughout the recipe development and writing process, I wouldn't have been able to get it all done without the support of my roommates, Karis Dodd, Michelle Cho, and Allison Garcia. Thank you for letting me monopolize our kitchen and living room for the greater part of a year to make this book happen. Thank you, Scott Newman, for couriering bags of Chester's Flamin' Hot Fries and offering a shoulder to cry on when I needed it the most. Thank you, Mariya Abdulkaf, for giving me advice on coordinating my photo shoot. To my friends and neighbors, Andrew Sisson and Laura Grasso, thank you for swinging by for extremely urgent taste tests.

Thank you to anyone who's tried my desserts, gone to my pop-ups, and shared my recipes. *Maraming salamat* to the Filipino community in New York, who has welcomed me with open arms. I cannot wait to keep having kamayan dinners together. Thank you to my coworkers at Bandsintown for cheering me on. To my food friends on the internet who I haven't even met IRL yet, thank you for sharing your creations and lives with the world. Your openness has inspired me to do the same with *The Dusky Kitchen*.

And last but not least, thank you, Jason Dessalet, for being my doting boyfriend and listening to me reread every section of my book aloud. I wouldn't have been able to deliver treat boxes without your mastery in logistics nor really start baking seriously in New York without you. I really appreciate the kindness and encouragement you and your family have shown me over these past few years. You are my #1 fan, and I don't know if I say this enough, but I love you.

**Matamis na Bao Alfajores
(Coconut Jam Shortbread Sandwich
Cookies; page 150)**

# INDEX

# ABOUT THE AUTHOR

**ABI BALINGIT** is the young, energetic Filipino American woman behind the blog *The Dusky Kitchen*. She made waves during the pandemic by selling pasalubong treat boxes filled with incredibly imaginative Filipino-inspired desserts and donating the proceeds to help those impacted by COVID-19. Her work has been covered by Thrillist, *Eater*, *Bon Appétit*, Food52, *Time Out*, *VICE*, and more. She lives in Brooklyn, New York.

theduskykitchen.com

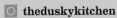 theduskykitchen

HarperCollins books may be purchased for educational, business, or sales promotional use. For information, please email the Special Markets Department at SPsales@harpercollins.com.

FIRST EDITION

*Designed by Leah Carlson-Stanisic*
*Photographs by Nico Schinco*
*Food Styling by Kaitlin Wayne*
*Prop Styling by Maeve Sheridan*
*Assistant Food Styling by Joy Cho*

---

Library of Congress Cataloging-in-Publication Data

Names: Balingit, Abi, author.

Title: Mayumu : Filipino American desserts remixed / Abi Balingit.

Description: First edition. | New York, NY: Harvest an Imprint of William Morrow, [2023] | Includes index.

Identifiers: LCCN 2022043527 | ISBN 9780063244061 (hardcover) | ISBN 9780063244085 (ebook)

Subjects: LCSH: Desserts. | Baking. | Filipino Americans--Food. | LCGFT: Cookbooks.

Classification: LCC TX773 .B2685 2023 | DDC 641.86--dc23/eng/20220920

LC record available at https://lccn.loc.gov/2022043527

---

ISBN 978-0-06-324406-1

23 24 25 26 27 GPS 10 9 8 7 6 5 4 3 2